ROMANS:
The
Gospel
According to
Paul

(A study of Romans 1–8)

Arden E. Gilmer

This book is intended for personal reading and also for group study. A teacher's guide is available from the publisher.

THE BRETHREN
PUBLISHING COMPANY
Ashland, Ohio

Library of Congress Catalog Card Number: 85-72274
ISBN: 0-934970-05-X

© 1985, The Brethren Publishing Company
Printed in the United States of America

THE BRETHREN PUBLISHING COMPANY
524 College Avenue, Ashland, Ohio 44805-3792

CONTENTS

About the author

Dr. Arden E. Gilmer is pastor of the Park Street Brethren Church, a congregation of approximately 425 members in Ashland, Ohio. Before going to Park Street in 1979, he was Director of Church Growth and Home Missions for The Brethren Church (1975-79), and prior to that he was pastor of the Pleasant View Brethren Church of Vandergrift, Pennsylvania (1968-75).

Dr. Gilmer has degrees from Ashland College (1965) and Ashland Theological Seminary (1968), and received a doctor of ministry degree from Fuller Theological Seminary in 1983. He and his wife, Roberta, are the parents of three sons.

Cover design by J. Howard Mack, Ashland, Ohio.

INTRODUCTION

I'm a throwback to the generation that took senior class trips. My high school class engaged in all kinds of projects to raise money to take a trip its senior year. The class was so small that we had to join with a senior class from another school to even qualify for group rates. But finally the day came and we boarded a train for the trip to New York City and Washington, D.C.

My biggest thrill on this trip was browsing through the National Archives in Washington. I enjoyed history, and there, carefully protected under glass and beautifully displayed, were the documents that played such a tremendously significant part in forming the United States and in directing its history.

I saw the Declaration of Independence, adopted by those brave patriots on July 4, 1776. Then there were the Articles of Confederation, followed by the Constitution of the United States of America and the subsequent Bill of Rights. (Do you remember memorizing the Preamble to the Constitution?). Working my way through the various exhibits, I eventually came to another special document, the Emancipation Proclamation, signed by President Abraham Lincoln on September 22, 1862. These are significant documents which altered the course of the history of our nation.

As we begin a journey through the first eight chapters of Paul's Letter to the Romans, we need to realize that we are dealing with one of the most significant documents ever written. An understanding of the message of this letter has transformed individual lives and revolutionized church history.

In the summer of A.D. 386, Aurelius Augustinus was under conviction to become a Christian but lacked the ability to make a final break with his old life of sin. One day he heard a child in a neighboring courtyard saying the words, "Take up and read! Take up and read!" He picked up a scroll and his eyes landed on Romans 13:13b-14: ". . . not in orgies and drunkenness, not in sexual immorality and debauchery, not in dissension and jealously. Rather, clothe yourselves with the Lord Jesus Christ, and do not think about how to gratify the desires of the sinful nature" (*NIV*). In his *Confessions* Augustine described his reaction: "No further would I read, nor had I any need; instantly, at the end of this sentence, a clear light flooded my heart, and all the darkness of doubt vanished away." Augustine became the most influential theologian of the church well into the Middle Ages.

The study of Romans also played a vital role in bringing about the period of church history known as the Reformation. When Martin Luther began teaching Romans to his theology students at the University of Wittenberg in 1515, he rediscovered the tremendous truth of justification by faith. Luther wrote, "Night and day I pondered until . . . I grasped the truth that the righteousness of God is that righteousness whereby, through grace and sheer mercy, he justifies us by faith. Thereupon I felt myself to be reborn and to have gone through open doors into paradise." The church of his day certainly was not honoring the doctrine of justification by faith which Luther discovered in Romans. His bold preaching of this truth was one of the forces of the Reformation.

Romans played a prominent role more than 200 years later in the conversion of another person who would become a dynamic man of God and a reforming force in the church of his time. In May 1738 John Wesley attended a service in a small church on Aldersgate Street in London. That evening someone was reading Luther's Preface to the Book of Romans. Wesley said that as he heard Luther's words, "I felt my heart strangely warmed. I felt I did trust in Christ, Christ alone, for my salvation; and an assurance was given me that he had taken **my** sins away, even **mine**; and saved me from the law of sin and death." Wesley went on to become a tireless worker for Christ and the driving force, the instrument of God, behind the 18th century Evangelical Revival.

The themes of Romans so enthralled John Bunyan as he studied the epistle while incarcerated in Bedford jail that he wrote *Pilgrim's Progress*, a classic in Christian literature. And the publication of Karl Barth's commentary on Romans was like a bombshell on the playground of the liberal theologians of several decades ago.

Romans was the driving force toward new insight and religious fervor in these and many other instances. If you do not experience accelerated spiritual pulse when you read and study Romans, you had better check the spiritual obituary column. Your name might be there. Romans is one of the most significant documents in the history of Christianity. If there is one book in the Bible whose contents you should master, Romans is it. Learn the outline of Romans, for it will help you share the message of salvation with others. Learn the themes of Romans. Explore them in depth. Your life will be renewed and enriched, and you will have much to share with others that will open their lives to the ways of God. Read Romans through in one sitting, then spend time in your devotions going back over it verse-by-verse, paragraph-by-paragraph, chapter-by-chapter, section-by-section.

The Book of Romans can rightly be called "The Gospel According to Paul." While Matthew, Mark, Luke, and John present the gospel as a historical account of the birth, life, activities, teaching, death, and resurrection of Jesus, Paul in Romans presents the gospel in the form of a theological treatise on the deep meanings and implications of the person and ministry of Jesus Christ. In fact, Paul uses the word "gospel" in the first verse of this epistle.

The gospel in Romans has long been recognized. Personal evangelists often teach people how to use the "Roman Road to Christ" (Rom. 3:23; 5:8; 6:23; 10:9, 10; 12:1, 2) as one way of explaining the plan of salvation. The Good News expounded by Paul is that Jesus Christ died and rose again to break the bondage of sin and death. Those who believe in Jesus Christ receive new spiritual life, and their relationship with God, destroyed by sin, is restored by God's grace. This new life expresses itself in consecrated Christian living as the Christian becomes more and more conformed to the image of Christ.

The Book of Romans satisfies the craving of the human spirit for a comprehensive exposition of the magnificent truths of salvation set forth in logical fashion. Salvation, the basic theme of Romans (see 1:16), is presented in terms of the righteousness of God, which, when received by faith, brings forth life. Nowhere else in the Bible is the subject of salvation presented with such thoroughness as in Romans. Thus the "Gospel According to Paul" is no misnomer as a subtitle for this epistle.

Paul wrote Romans in the early part of A.D. 57, as he completed his winter in Corinth. By this time he had finished his missionary journeys through the eastern part of the Mediterranean world. He had been preaching for nearly 25 years and had already penned a letter to the Galatians, two epistles to the Thessalonians, and two to the Corinthians. He was not a Christian novice when the Holy Spirit anointed him to write this masterpiece. In fact, he would soon begin his final journey to Jerusalem, where he would be arrested. He had a tremendous desire to go to Rome, the capital of the great Roman Empire (see Romans 1:11-13). He would eventually arrive in Rome, but as a prisoner rather than as free traveler.

Since Paul had carried the gospel to most of the eastern part of the Mediterranean world, he began to look zealously for new frontiers into which he could spread the Good News. His eyes fell on the western Mediterranean countries. As he planned his work in the west, he needed a base of operations similar to the church at Antioch, which had served as his base in the east. The church at Rome was an ideal location.

But Paul had never visited Rome. Therefore he wanted the church there to know the exact nature of the message he preached. Perhaps other visitors to Rome, among them critics of Paul, had misrepresented his preaching. To counteract any such misrepresentation, he wrote a precise treatise of the gospel he preached. In Paul's letters to churches which he had founded, he dealt with specific problems within those congregations. But in his letter to the church at Rome, he deals with the subject of salvation. His thorough treatment of this subject serves in a sense as a letter of introduction, so that the Roman Christians could receive him with open arms and then give him their support as he took the Gospel of Christ to the west.

Perhaps as Paul wrote Romans he had a Holy Spirit inspired premonition that things would turn against him when he reached Jerusalem. What if he should not live to declare the gospel in the west? "Then he must write a letter so systematic and comprehensive that the church would be able intelligently to continue his work, proclaiming the very gospel he was spelling out for them, taking it in his stead to the farthest reaches of the empire. For all he knew at the time, this letter might be in a sense his last will and testament, a precious deposit bequested to the church and through it to the community of the faithful everywhere."[1]

No wonder Romans has been such a powerful missionary document and tool throughout all the ages of the church! In Romans Paul compressed the essence of his missionary preaching — the message that had resulted in the conversion of multitudes of people and the establishment of scores of churches. The critics who would attempt to discredit Paul by twisting or adulterating his message would now be measured by what he himself had put into writing. Faulty misconceptions could now be corrected. Adulterations could be weighed and their errors exposed. Missionary communication now had a new lodestar — The Epistle to the Romans.

The following chapters are based on a series of expository sermons on Romans that I preached at the Park Street Brethren Church in Ashland, Ohio, from September 1981 through July 1982. The content of most chapters is based on edited transcriptions of those messages. The style, therefore, is more conversational than might be the case if the manuscripts had been prepared from the beginning for publication purposes.

Preparing and preaching this series of sermons enriched and edified my life immeasureably. I pray that your life will also be rejuvenated and expanded as you work through this study, either individually or with others in a class. May the evangelistic and missionary zeal of both the Holy Spirit and the Apostle Paul be implanted in your heart so deeply that it will take root, sprout, and bring forth much fruit, as new citizens join the Kingdom of Christ. May you, like Paul, declare with new vigor, "I am not ashamed of the gospel!"

Many have contributed to these messages through their writings which I have read, their sermons which I have heard, their participation in Bible studies of which I have been a part, and their countless conversations with me (by both Christians and non-Christians). Some of these contributions I cannot precisely document because they have become a part of the fabric of my life. Others I can document, and where possible, I have done so. Ultimately, all praise and thanks go to the triune God, who initiated, accomplished, and sustains our salvation.

DR. ARDEN E. GILMER
Ashland, Ohio

PRELUDE
TO THE EPISTLE

CHAPTER ONE

GOD'S WHOLEHEARTED SERVANT
Romans 1:1-17

PEOPLE of different cultures have their own ways of greeting one another, of saying "Hello." In the United States, we usually greet one another with a handshake and a "Hello, how are you doin'?" If the greeting is between close friends, it may even include a warm embrace.

People from most oriental cultures, however, greet each other not with a handshake, but by each person placing his hands together in front of his chest, then bowing politely to the other person. Recently one of our church's teenagers was showing me another way of saying "Hello" by trying to teach me the "soul" handshake. It was too complicated for me, but it's a very special way by which members of another cultural group greet one another.

Paul Introduces Himself

The way of saying "Hello" in written communication also varies from culture to culture. In verse one of Romans, Paul follows the customary form of his day for greeting someone in a letter. He begins by introducing himself so that the recipients of the letter will know immediately the identity of the writer. (Compare the first verses of Paul's other New Testament epistles). In Romans, Paul is introducing himself to a church he had never visited, so his greeting is somewhat more terse than his greetings to some of the churches with which he was more familiar.

After giving his name, Paul uses three phrases to introduce himself to the Roman Christians. First, he calls himself "a bond-servant of Christ Jesus." The word translated "bond-servant" is the strongest of the Greek words for servant, and literally means slave. The bond slave was one who had no will of his own. He was completely controlled by his master. Whatever the master said had to be done. The bond slave did not question his master. He simply obeyed.

All Christians are to be slaves of Christ. Through His great love for us, He purchased us. The price He paid was His own blood (cf. I Pet. 1:18, 19). Our slavery is grounded in love — His for us and ours in return to Him for His redemptive work in our lives.

The Old Testament tells about the "love slave." If a Hebrew was in debt, he could sell himself as a slave to another Hebrew. But that slavery would last only six years at the maximum. During the seventh year, the Sabbath year, the slave would be given his freedom and also some provisions so that he could begin his economic life again.

But there was another option. Perhaps during the period of slavery, a love relationship developed between the slave and his master. If so, the person who had sold himself into slavery had the option to continue by his own choice to be a slave of that master. He then became a slave motivated by love rather than a slave motivated by necessity. To symbolize the new relationship, the slave's ear was pierced. For the rest of his life he would be a love slave to that master (Deut. 15:12-17).

Isn't this a beautiful picture of our relationship with Jesus Christ? He loves us, and we say "Yes" to Him and want to serve Him as Lord of our lives. Paul had this kind of relationship with Jesus Christ. Do you?

Second, Paul introduces himself as an apostle. An apostle is literally a person sent on a mission. Jesus used the verbal form of this word to refer to his being sent by God. Our term missionary describes the function of an apostle. But an apostle also had a unique position because he was "called" by God. Paul received his call to apostleship at the time of his conversion (Acts 26:12-18), and this was later confirmed by the Lord through the ministry of Ananias (Acts 9:15-18). Paul began fulfilling his new position immediately (Acts 9:20).

All Christians are to function as people sent from God on a unique mission. We are His witnesses. However, we are not all called to the position of apostle. Instead we are "called to belong to Jesus Christ" and "to be saints" (Rom. 1:6, 7; *NIV*).

Third, Paul introduces himself as one "set apart for the gospel of God." Knowing this — that he had been set aside for the gospel — Paul could concentrate wholeheartedly on this ministry. He did not spend time daydreaming: "What if I were a business executive making a big salary and receiving big bonuses? What if I were a multimillion-dollar professional sports superstar?" Paul was not distracted by hypothetical "what if" questions. He knew his calling and he put all of his energy into fulfilling it.

Do you know your calling as a Christian? For what purpose in particular have you been set apart? God by his grace has equipped you with some spiritual gift which sets you apart for some ministry. Do you know what it is? Paul did, and each of us should, too.

Paul Declares the Gospel

The gospel was so much a part of Paul's life that he cannot introduce himself to the Romans without also declaring that gospel. He doesn't even conclude the first verse before mentioning it. He says (by way of summary) that it is "the gospel of God" [v. 1] . . . concerning His Son [v. 3] . . . Jesus Christ our Lord [v. 4]."

The Good News is what God has done for us in Jesus Christ. Christianity is not a religion. Christianity is Christ! The uniqueness of Christianity is the uniqueness of Jesus Christ. Paul expresses this uniqueness in several ways (vv. 2-4).

First, the gospel of Jesus Christ is the culmination of God's promises (v. 2). The gospel proclaimed by Paul was deeply rooted in the Old Testament scriptures from the promise to Adam and Eve in Genesis 3:15 to the promise of the Sun of Righteousness in Malachi 4:2. Jesus Christ was God's fulfillment of all the Old Testament's expectations of a coming deliverer.

Second, the uniqueness of Jesus Christ is expressed in a brief statement about His two natures. When Jesus came as the promised Messiah, He was both human and divine. On the human side, He had a family tree. He was a descendant of David. The genealogies given by both Matthew and Luke demonstrate His human ancestry.

But Jesus Christ in His incarnation was not only the Son of

David, He was also the Son of God. His divine Sonship was powerfully demonstrated by His resurrection from the dead (v. 4). His resurrection proved the authenticity of His claim to be *the* Son of God. The gospel is unique because its central person is unique. No other person ever has been or ever will be 100 percent human and 100 percent divine. But Jesus was and is. No other leader of any world religion or cult has ever risen from the dead, but Jesus did, and He is alive forevermore. "According to the Spirit" (v. 4) shows that all three persons of the Trinity were essential to and active in the fulfillment of God's gospel. Because of the uniqueness of Jesus and His gospel, Paul rightly calls him "Lord" (v. 4).

Paul Defines His Ministry

After sharing the uniqueness of the gospel, Paul moves on to define his ministry (vv. 5, 6). Notice how his ministry flowed right out of the person and work of Jesus Christ. The same is true of the church collectively and of Christians individually. Paul never forgot what happened to him on the Damascus Road (Acts 9:1-9). The living Christ stopped him dead in his tracks and engulfed him in redemptive light. Paul called that grace, for it was undeserved. In another place Paul called himself the chief of sinners and, therefore, totally undeserving of God's favor. Yet God "graced" him not only by saving him but also by calling him to the important ministry of apostleship. Paul experienced both kinds of grace — the grace that saves (Eph. 2:8, 9) and the grace that equips those who are saved so that they become servants (I Cor. 15:9, 10).

Paul's service was apostleship. Yours may be something else. But God has "graced" all Christians, and we must be faithful in ministry. Paul's ministry was God's gift to him. The scope of his ministry was "all the Gentiles" or "all the nations" (v. 5). The purpose of his ministry was to bring people to the obedience of faith. Paul's preaching was incomplete until people obeyed the gospel by believing in and committing their lives to Jesus Christ. We, too, must not only share the gospel but also call people to faith and obedience so that new converts become responsible ministering members of the church.

Paul concludes his salutation with his customary "grace and peace" statement (v. 7; cf. I Cor. 1:3; II Cor. 1:2; Gal. 1:3; Eph. 1:2; Phil. 1:2; Col. 1:2; I Thess. 1:1; II Thess. 1:2; I Tim.

1:2; II Tim. 1:2). He took seven verses to say "Hello." But these verses are loaded with the essentials of the gospel. If these verses were the only scripture we had, we would know who Jesus Christ is, that He accomplished "good news" for us, that we must say "Yes" in faith to His saving work for us, and that we, as Christians, are to be constantly involved in His service.

After introducing himself, Paul continues the personal touch by expressing his appreciation for the Roman Christians (vv. 8-12). Paul customarily included words of appreciation for those to whom he was writing, especially applauding their faith. Along with praise for the believers he gives assurance that he is diligently praying for them. Even though he had never been to Rome, he was nevertheless constant and regular in his prayers for the Roman believers. Thus far this appreciation was based upon what he had heard. It was appreciation from a distance. But Paul had an intense longing to be with them in person. So his prayers included petitions that he would eventually have the opportunity to visit them.

Indeed, Paul had made plans several times to go to Rome. But something had always interferred. He explains his intense desire to see them in verses 11-12. He believed that both he and the church would gain spiritually from such a face to face visit. Each had something to give to the other which would result in mutual encouragement and upbuilding for all. Even though Paul was a pioneer, he was no "Lone Ranger" Christian. He had an intense desire for relationships with other Christians and was well aware that he benefited from them. All Christians need to share more often their words of appreciation for each other. Often we are quick to criticize but slow to compliment. Paul provides an excellent model for both pastors and parishioners in this regard. Express appreciation to someone today.

Paul Explains His Motivation
Paul claimed that he served God with his "whole heart in preaching the gospel of his Son" (v. 9, *NIV*). Wholehearted service is the fruit of intense motivations. Paul was driven, and he explains his motivations in verses 13-17. Understanding Paul's motivations will make it possible for us to measure our own. Paul was a high achiever for Jesus Christ. Today it's fashionable to cut down a high achiever by calling him a

workaholic. But the scriptures constantly exhort us to be zealous, diligent, and faithful in our ministry. Paul was, and as a
result he accomplished many magnificent things for the Lord.
What motivated him?

A Man of Vision

First, he was a man of **vision** (v. 13). Every high achiever
has a vision, and all his energy is channeled into making that
vision a reality. People of faith are people of vision. They see
with the eye of faith the possibilities contained in God's promises long before they become experiential reality. Vision looks
beyond today to the multitude of tomorrows. Vision turns
negative thinkers who see only problems into possibility
thinkers, energized with a "can do" attitude, who work for
solutions. Vision fosters perseverance. A person with a vision
will not give up no matter how many obstacles may arise.

The nature of our vision is of essential importance because
it determines our thoughts and actions. Early one morning a
man took a walk around a lake. He came upon a man fishing
and paused to watch him. Soon the man had a bite. He reeled
in the fish, took it off the hook, and held it up to a stick which
was about seven inches long. The fish was longer than the
stick, so the man threw it back into the lake. This baffled the
watcher, so he continued to observe the fisherman. He caught
several more fish and measured each one by that seven-inch
stick. If the fish was shorter than the stick, he kept it. If it
was longer, he threw it back.

This seemed totally backward to the observer, so he approached the fisherman. "Why do you keep the small ones and
throw back the big ones?" he asked.

The fisherman replied, "I have a seven-inch frying pan!"

This fisherman's actions were determined by his small vision. He had a seven-inch frying pan vision. Because of his
small vision, he was throwing the big ones back. How many
times have you missed God's bigger possibilities because you
had such a small vision. Ephesians 3:20-21 should expand
your vision.

Paul was a man with a tremendous vision, and that vision
motivated him to go via Rome to take the gospel to Spain.
Paul had a definite vision: "that I might obtain some fruit
among you also, even as among the rest of the Gentiles [na-
tions]" (v. 13). His vision was of a people ripe for spiritual har-

vest. His vision was the same as his Lord's (cf. Jn. 4:35).

Many churches will respond to a concrete vision, for example constructing a new church building or adding new Sunday school rooms. The members work hard and give well because they can see the vision become reality and they can see the fruits of their labors. But quite frankly, most churches are not putting the same kind of commitment of time, energy, and money into making the spiritual vision — a harvest of souls for the Kingdom of God — a reality. We are too dependent on instant gratification. We need to develop Paul's kind of spiritual vision of non-Christians becoming Christians. Our actions (or inaction) clearly reveal that we do not share Paul's vision. Therefore, our motivation is shallow.

A Man Under Obligation

In verses 14-16 Paul gives three more sources of his motivation, each of them set forth in an "I am" statement. First, he writes, "I am under obligation . . ." (v. 14). Paul owed someone something. Therefore, he was in debt. To whom was Paul in debt? One would think that he would say, "I am in debt to God. I owe so much to God. He saved me. He redeemed me. He is in my life everyday. He has given me new life in Christ."

Paul would agree with these statements. But here he took another approach. He said that he had an obligation to a wide diversity of people: Greeks, barbarians, the wise, and the foolish. He covered the extremes of the human spectrum of his day in order to include all. He had a duty to people he had not yet met. He had a duty to share with them the Good News of Jesus Christ (v. 9). As a Christian who had experienced God's redeeming work in his life, Paul was honor bound to make sure that all people had the opportunity to hear about Jesus Christ and to believe in him. As a Christian he had a **duty** to obey the commands of Christ, including the one which said, "Go into all the world and make disciples of all the nations." If Paul did not fulfill his duty, he was disobedient to His Lord and lost his integrity as a servant of Jesus Christ. Duty born of integrity motivated Paul. We, likewise, should be so motivated.

Paul revealed his third motivational secret in verse 15: "I am eager to preach the gospel . . . ." With this statement Paul moved beyond duty to **attitude**. Paul understood his duty and said, "I am ready. I am avid. I am zealous. I have the joy of

the Lord and His salvation in my spirit, and as a result I'm
full of enthusiasm. I can't wait to share the Good News." Duty
without joy and anticipation soon becomes drudgery. Sadly,
for some Christians, life has become a joyless drudge. They
may occasionally fulfill their duty, but they receive no joy
from it.

But Paul knew that there was joy in serving Jesus and in
sharing the gospel. Because his attitude was one of serving
the Lord with gladness, he could sing joyful praises at mid-
night in the jail at Philippi even though his body was throb-
bing with pain from the beating received earlier in the day.

Several years ago the Kansas City, Missouri, police depart-
ment received a call that a man had climbed the steel
superstructure of one of the bridges crossing the Missouri
River and was threatening to jump. Sergeant Richard Huddle
answered the call. With safety belt in place he made his way
toward the man. As he approached, the man jumped. The
sergeant, responding instantly, also jumped toward the man,
caught him in midair and saved his life.

Since our instantaneous responses often reveal our real attitudes, we can say that this policeman was not motivated
only by duty. He liked people, and because of this attitude he
responded even without thinking about possible danger to
himself in order to save a life. How are you fulfilling your
Christian duty? Knowing the joy of the Lord is a powerful and
positive motivation.

A Man of Conviction

Paul's third "I am" statement gives his fourth motivational
secret: "I am not ashamed of the gospel . . ." (v. 16). In this
statement Paul's foundational **conviction** thunders forth. By
the time Paul wrote these words, he had been hounded out of
Damascus for preaching the gospel. He had been stoned and
left for dead in Lystra. He had been jailed in Philippi. The
philosophers of Athens had jeered him. But even after endur-
ing such tremendous opposition, Paul would not quit. Why?
The bedrock of his ministry was his conviction about the gospel. Why was he so unwavering in his conviction? He tells us:
"it is the power of God for salvation to every one who believes
. . ." (v. 16).

We live in a power-oriented society today. We hear about
nuclear power, electric power, oil power, political power,

economic power, etc. Power, power, power. But among all these you cannot find a single power that can save a human soul. Only one power in all the universe can do that, and it's the power of the gospel. The word "power" used here denotes an inherent quality of the gospel itself. It's not something that the church fabricates and puts into the gospel. It's a power that God Himself has put into the gospel. Only one power can forgive sin, break the bondage of Satan and death, and change lives.

> *There is pow'r, pow'r,*
> *Wonderworking power*
> *In the precious blood of the Lamb.*

Paul knew this power personally. It had liberated him. He had witnessed this power transform countless other lives. As a result, he boldly declared without reservation, "I am not ashamed of the gospel." Do you share a similar conviction about the gospel? You will have little motivation for witness without it.

Vision, duty, attitude, and conviction — four motivations that caused Paul to be a high achiever for Christ and a wholehearted servant of the Lord. I hope that you are also wholeheartedly serving the Lord. If you're not, what changes do you need to make? This passage is loaded with ideas. Consider them.

QUESTIONS FOR DISCUSSION

1. How did the form of a letter in Paul's culture differ from the form of a letter in our culture? What do you think of the idea of the writer putting his name at the beginning of the letter (rather than at the end)?
2. How do you react to the idea of being a "love slave" to Jesus Christ?
3. What does this statement (from the text) mean: "The uniqueness of Christianity is the uniqueness of Christ"? Do you agree with the statement?
4. How does our vision influence our accomplishments?
5. To what extent are Paul's four motivations — vision, duty, attitude, conviction — found in your church? In your life? Is any one of them more lacking than the others?

UNIT ONE

ALL ARE GUILTY BEFORE GOD

CHAPTER TWO

CONSEQUENCES OF DEMOTING GOD

Romans 1:18-32

IN verse 18 of chapter one of Romans, Paul begins his formal exposition of the gospel that he had preached throughout the Mediterranean world. He believed that this gospel had been revealed to him by no less than Jesus Christ, so he calls it the gospel of God's Son (1:9). In the first part of his exposition of this gospel (1:18—3:20), Paul plays the role of a prosecuting attorney. It's as though all of mankind are in a court of law, and Paul is presenting God's case against them. But in doing so, he also opens the door for the pardon that mankind needs, which has been supplied by God in the Gospel of Jesus Christ.

In the first paragraph (1:18–32) of this section, the Apostle Paul describes the Gentile world as he knew it in his day. But as we read through this paragraph, we discover that there are many similarities between the Gentile world of Paul's day and the world today outside of Jesus Christ. (*If you have not already done so, take a few minutes now to read this paragraph — Romans 1:18–32 — before reading on.*)

Natural Revelation

In these verses, Paul describes for us how man demotes God and the consequences of doing so. He begins by explaining that God has revealed Himself to all of mankind. Therefore, all persons are without excuse.

Paul is focusing here on what theologians call natural revelation, that is, the revelation God gives of Himself in the natural world — in the universe, the cosmos. There is order in the world in which we live, and that order points to someone who created it. The design in this world points to someone who designed it — a Master Designer.

It's interesting that people will look at a watch and not argue that somebody designed and made that watch. No one even suggests that it came into being by mere chance — that as the result of a process that took millions of years the parts came floating together to suddenly become a watch. But just as the watch points to a watchmaker, so the natural world points to a designer. It points to one who caused the whole world to come into being.

Paul says that the visible world is a witness, a testimony to the invisible attributes of God, namely His power, His majesty, His supremacy, and His glory. This, of course, was not a new idea with Paul. Centuries earlier the Psalmist had described how the heavens reveal God's glory to mankind.

> The heavens are telling of the glory of God;
> And their expanse is declaring the work of His hands.
> Day to day pours forth speech,
> And night to night reveals knowledge.
> There is no speech, nor are there words;
> Their voice is not heard.
>
> Psalm 19:1-3

Through natural revelation — in this case the daily journey of the sun and moon around our planet — the glory of God is declared. Since they do not use any human language, no language barrier is involved. People from all over the world observe the sun rising and the sun setting. If they really understood nature, they would comprehend the glory and the majesty of God. Nature would be a revelation of God to them.

Natural Revelation Perverted

God in His grace has granted all mankind this revelation of Himself. But instead of honoring God and giving Him the glory for what He has done, man, motivated by his sinful heart and his rebellion against God, has taken that natural revelation and perverted it. He has demoted God and made God more like himself. Indeed, he has placed God under himself. Man's heresy is that he worships the creature rather than the Creator.

Notice how Paul describes this. He says that men despised the revelation of God. This involved an act of the will. They willfully turned against the revelation of God that He had given them in the natural world. They did not see God functioning in all of this. We have people today just like that, don't we? They do not see God, His marvels, His glory, and His power in the meticulous design of the natural world. As Elizabeth Barrett Browning wrote:

> Earth's crammed with heaven,
> And every common bush afire with God;
> But only he who sees, takes off his shoes,
> The rest sit round it and pluck blackberries . . .

A person's orientation is determined by the condition of his heart. While some people despise the revelation of God in nature, others worship God and find His glory revealed there.

But what about those who don't honor Him as God and who instead give His glory to idols? The Apostle Paul declares, "They are without excuse" (v. 20). They are defenseless. When they stand before God, they won't be able to plead that they didn't know, that they had no revelation. The natural world gave them a significant revelation, pointing them to God's power and glory. But in their sin, they perverted that revelation. Verse 25 identifies their basic heresy: They worshiped and served the creature rather than the Creator.

In Paul's day this heresy was expressed in the sin of idolatry. At first, the ungodly started making idols in the likeness of man. But as their degeneration continued, they made idols in the likeness of birds and four-footed animals and reptiles.

Humanism—Modern-Day Idolatry

Is idolatry still with us? Does our sophisticated 20th century, with all of its technology, science, and behavioral sciences, have any idols? Is there any instance where we worship the creature rather than the Creator? Yes, we have at least one idol in our world. It's epitomized by the philosophy known as Humanism. Writing it "huMANism" pinpoints the central feature of this philosophy — MAN.

We Christians understand that man is a creature. He is not the Creator. But in Humanism, man has nearly become deified. Humanism is the idolatry of our age. Ancient astronomers believed that the sun, moon, and stars revolved around the earth. Copernicus had a long battle convincing his generation that the earth actually revolved around the sun. In a similar way, many today believe that the "world" revolves around man. They refuse to acknowledge that the world actually revolves around God.

Basic Tenets of Humanism

Humanism is propagated through *The Humanist* magazine. Two manifestoes — written in 1933 and 1973 — state its basic tenets. Tim LaHaye in his book, *Battle for the Mind*, summarizes the Humanists beliefs into five categories.[1]

The first of these is *atheism*. Humanists state: "We find insufficient evidence for belief in the existence of the supernatural . . . as nontheists we begin with man not God . . . no deity will save us; we must save ourselves." Doesn't that sound like worship of the creature rather than the Creator?

From atheism Humanists move to evolution. "Religious Humanists regard the universe as self-existing and not created. . . . the human species is an emergence from natural evolutionary forces." It takes more faith to believe in evolution than it takes to believe the Bible.

The third tenet of Humanism is *amorality* — not morality or immorality — but amorality. They say, "Ethics is autonomous and situational . . . ." In other words, the situation determines our ethical response. There are no absolutes, no supernatural moral code that man is commanded to obey. Instead, ethics stem from self-interest. Humanists favor the right to birth control, abortion, divorce, and choice of sex direction. In other words, whatever pleases the person is "A-OK."

The forth tenet of Humanism is *autonomous, self-created man*. "We believe in maximum individual autonomy — reject all religious, moral codes that suppress freedom . . . demand civil liberties, including right to oppose governmental policies — right to die with dignity, euthanasia and suicide." The final authority is man, not God. If a person decides that the best for him is to take his life, he should be allowed to commit suicide.

The fifth tenet of Humanism is a *socialist one-world view*. They say, "We have reached a turning point in human history where the best often is to transcend the limits of national sovereignty and move toward the building of a world community . . . the peaceful adjudication of differences by international courts." They want a one-world government. They believe that man can create his own Utopia and that this one-world government could solve all problems.

These basic tenets of humanism clearly make man the center. Humanism worships the creature rather than the Creator. Someone has summed it up in a little poem called "The Humanist."[2]

> He exists because he was created.
> He's here because he was placed here.
> He's well and comfortable because divine power keeps
>   him so.
> He dines at God's table.
> He's sheltered by the roof that God gave him.
> He's clothed by God's bounty.
> He lives by breathing God's air which keeps him strong
>   and vocal to go about persuading people that whether
>   God is or not, only man matters.

The Humanist uses all of the bounties of God to go against God. That's the way man demotes God. Instead of worshiping the Creator, "who is blessed forever" (v. 25), he worships the creature.

"God Gave Them Over"

The Apostle Paul goes on to itemize several consequences of man demoting God. These consequences are indicated by the phrase "God gave them over." God gave the ungodly over to several different things. Paul states the first of these in verse 24: "Therefore God gave them over in the lusts of their hearts to impurity, that their bodies might be dishonored among them." The first step in the degradation of the ungodly, then, is the realization of their hearts' desire. God said, "If that's their hearts' desire, I'll let them have it." God does this by way of punishment. According to verse 18, this is an expression of the "wrath of God."

You know, at times there's nothing worse than for me to have my heart's desire. Somebody needs to say there's a higher good than my heart's desire. But to the ungodly, God just says, "OK, we'll remove any aspiration for a higher good. That's the way they want it. They can have their hearts' desire." And when this happens, the first step is sexual impurity. I don't think I need to go into detail about everything that's happening in our culture in this area.

The second time Paul says, "God gave them over," is in

verses 26 and 27. In these verses man moves one step down the degradation ladder. As a result of worshiping the creature rather than the Creator, man goes from sexual impurity to sexual perversion. Paul clearly states that homosexuality is a consequence of the sin of the ungodly and of their worship of the creature rather than the Creator.

Remember that Humanists say there should be no mandates, no higher power to dictate sex direction. According to them, if a person finds fulfillment being a homosexual, then he should have the right to practice homosexuality. But God's word calls this sexual depravity, because it replaces the natural desire that God intended with that which is unnatural. Some people today look at biblical passages and try to demonstrate that the Bible permits covenant homosexual relationships. I, for the life of me, cannot see how they can do this. The Apostle Paul clearly labels homosexuality as depravity.

This is not to say, however, that the homosexual person is without hope. Christ died for the homosexual just as he died for the thief, the adulterer, and the murderer. But His death for homosexuals does not make the homosexual lifestyle acceptable in God's sight. God gave man over to that. God said, "Have your own way. Do whatever you want." Homosexuality was the punishment.

In verse 28 Paul goes on to say, "God gave them over to a depraved mind . . . ." I haven't mentioned it yet, but the word exchange is used several times in this passage. In verse 23 Paul says that the ungodly "exchanged the glory of the incorruptible God for an image in the form of corruptible man . . . ." In verse 25 he says that they "exchanged the truth of God for a lie." In verses 26 and 27 he says that both men and women "exchanged the natural function for that which is unnatural."

Though the word "exchange" is not used in verse 28, the idea is there nevertheless. The ungodly exchanged an understanding of the knowledge of God for a depraved mind. A depraved mind is one that is unable to make ethical distinctions, judgments, and discernments. A depraved mind has no conscience. A depraved mind cannot understand spiritual things because it has traveled so long the treadmill of worshiping the creature rather than the Creator. As a result, it simply loses its ability to discern what is right and what is wrong. All of the sins mentioned in verses 29–31 are evidences of the depraved mind. The last four, those mentioned in verse 31, sum it up. The depraved mind is "senseless, faithless, heartless, ruthless" (*NIV*).

Steve Turner, a free-lance journalist, has written a book of poetry entitled *Nice and Nasty*. In one poem, he satirizes the warped thinking of our age:[3]

Creed

We believe in Marxfreudanddarwin.
We believe everything is OK
as long as you don't hurt anyone,
to the best of your definition of hurt,
and to the best of your knowledge.

We believe in sex before during
and after marriage.
We believe in the therapy of sin.
We believe that adultery is fun.
We believe that sodomy's OK.
We believe that taboos are taboo.

We believe that everything's getting better
despite evidence to the contrary.
The evidence must be investigated.
You can prove anything with evidence.

We believe there's something in horoscopes,
ufo's and bent spoons;
Jesus was a good man just like Buddha
Mohammed and ourselves.
He was a good moral teacher although we think
his good morals were bad.

We believe that all religions are basically the same,
at least the one that we read was.
They all believe in love and goodness.
They only differ on matters of
creation sin heaven hell God and salvation.

We believe that after death comes The Nothing
because when you ask the dead what happens
they say Nothing.
If death is not the end, if the dead have lied,
then it's compulsory heaven for all
excepting perhaps Hitler, Stalin, and Genghis Khan.

We believe in Masters and Johnson.
What's selected is average.
What's average is normal.
What's normal is good.

*   *   *   *   *

We believe that man is essentially good.
It's only his behavior that lets him down.
This is the fault of society.
Society is the fault of conditions.
Conditions are the fault of society.

We believe that each man must find the truth
that is right for him.
Reality will adapt accordingly.
The universe will readjust. History will alter.
We believe that there is no absolute truth
excepting the truth that there is no absolute truth.

We believe in the rejection of creeds,
and the flowering of individual thought.

Tragically, this is a fairly accurate description of the beliefs
of many today. This poem points out some of the flaws and
blind spots in worldly thinking. But people are blind to the
blind spots. Paul says in verse 32, ". . . although they know
the ordinance of God, that those who practice such things are
worthy of death, they not only do the same, but also give
hearty approval to those who practice them." They know what
they are doing is worthy of death. They have the revelation of
God. But in spite of that, they not only do these things, but
they are their own cheering section. They applaud each
other's wrong doings.

Charles Colson, in an article that appeared in the October
2, 1981, issue of *Christianity Today*, reminds us that we live
in "A Society that Celebrates Sin." He asks us to consider the
case of John Jenrette, who as a congressman from South
Carolina fell into the net of the FBI's Abscam investigation,
was convicted of taking a bribe, defeated for re-election, and
sentenced to prison.

Jenrette's wife, Rita, rather than stick by her husband, saw
this as a situation she could exploit to her own financial advantage. For a large sum of money she posed in the buff for a
well-known men's magazine. She also divorced her husband.

And how did our society respond to her actions? She was
given interview after interview by both the print media and
by talk show hosts. Luncheons in her honor were held in the
poshest clubs.

How did Paul say it? "They give hearty approval to those
who practice these things" (v. 32).

One interviewer asked Mrs. Jenrette how she could justify
skipping out on her marriage when her husband was going

through a difficult time. Her response was, "I've paid my dues." This caused Colson to ask, "When do we ever pay our dues for commitment, once revered as sacred? She threw off her marriage as easily as she threw off her undergarments for the photographers. . . . And then we made her a genuine celebrity, to the lustful cheers of millions of males and the applause of some feminists who admired her courage."

Obviously, Paul was not only describing the first century Gentile world. His characterization sounds very contemporary. It all happens when man demotes God. The root mistake — worshiping the creature rather than the Creator.

How Shall We Respond?

What's our response to this? What was the Apostle Paul's response? Some Christians talk about how bad our world is and they tell us to crawl off into a corner until Jesus comes. That was not Paul's approach. He realistically described the paganism, the depravity, the sin of his world. But how did he begin his response? He declared, "I am not ashamed of the gospel" (v. 16). Why? Because "it is the power of God for salvation to every one who believes" (v. 16). In this gospel "the righteousness of God is revealed" (v. 17).

What did a world like Paul's need? It needed a revelation of the righteousness of God. And where is that revelation? Paul said it's in the gospel — in the Gospel of Jesus Christ. I'm not ashamed of that gospel, he declared. That gospel must go forward. It is the only hope of the world.

Yes, Paul's description gives an accurate picture of the world in which we live and of some of the thinking of that world. But that doesn't mean that we should crawl into a corner and pull our Christian covers over our heads. Instead, we, with Paul, must say, "I'm not ashamed of the gospel." It's the only spiritual medicine that will cure the sin and the depravity of the world in which we live.

QUESTIONS FOR DISCUSSION

1. What are some other ways (in addition to those mentioned) that nature reveals God? What is revealed about God?
2. To what extent has Humanism influenced our schools, television, radio, and the print media?
3. How can we best combat the depravity in our world? What was Paul's approach?

CHAPTER THREE

WHAT ABOUT
THE MORALIST?

Romans 2:1-16

W E are now in the section of Romans in which Paul demonstrates that every human being has a need before God. That need is created by sin and can be met, as Paul will tell us later, only by salvation through faith in Jesus Christ. In this section Paul writes in great detail about different categories of the human race in order to show that each of them is guilty before God. As you recall from the previous lesson, Paul, in the last half of chapter 1, painted a vivid picture of the rampant sin in the pagan world. After stating the basic flaw of the pagan world, he presented the consequences of that flaw in a list of 23 perversions and vile sins.

Faults of the Moralist

At the beginning of chapter 2, Paul writes as if he is speaking before an audience. As he speaks about the views of the pagans, he spots a critic in the audience who says, "Yes, Paul, that's true of some people. But I'm not like that. True, I have no faith in Christ, but I'm very moral in my lifestyle. I'm a clean-cut young chap. Who could find fault with me." In Romans 2:1-16 Paul answers the objections of this person. He speaks to the person of high moral values and shows how God views him and his need for Christ.

In this passage, then, Paul answers the question, "What about the moralist?" He deals with those who are moral in the Gentile world as well as with those Jews who are exceptionally moral in their lifestyle. He points out the faults of the moralist, and in so doing he brings forth the principles by which God judges mankind. Paul's explanation of God's criteria of judgment underlines the basic faults of the moralist.

Moralists Are Pretentious

What are the faults of the moralist? To begin with, moralists are pretentious (2:1-3). They make a public show of doing certain things, but behind the scenes they do not live up to that which they profess. They are two-faced. They do not practice what they preach. Indeed, they go around judging other people on the basis of moral standards that they themselves do not live by.

The pagan world had some very fine moralists. One of the pagan philosophers who was something of a moralist was a contemporary of the Apostle Paul. His name was Seneca. He was a tutor of the Roman Emperor Nero. As a Stoic, he represented the moral side of pagan philosophy. In his writings, Seneca exalted high moral virtues. He rediculed vulgar idolatry. He exposed hypocrisy and saw the pervasive character of evil. He wrote, "All vices exist in all men, though all vices do not stand out prominently in each man." He taught that people should practice daily self-examination. For those who read his writings, he assumed the role of moral guide.

But Seneca is an illustration of Paul's point. Though he wrote great moral teaching, he did not in every instance live up to that which he taught. In fact, one of his most flagrant sins was participating in Nero's conspiracy to kill the emperor's mother.

So the problem with the moralist is that he is incapable of living up to that which he teaches. He cannot practice what he preaches. But Paul says this is what every moralist must do if he's going to be genuine. If not, he is two-faced.

But this was not a problem of only the Gentile moralist. Jesus dealt with Jewish people who were like this. Many of them belonged to the sect of the Pharisees. These Pharisees were vehement in their judgment of other people. They looked down on other people if they failed to obey the most trifling ritualistic detail.

Jesus told a parable on one occasion about two men who went to the Temple to pray (Lk. 18:9-14). One was a sinner, and he prayed only for the mercy of God in his life. But the other was a Pharisee. He prayed, "God, I thank Thee that I'm not like this other person." He had a moral lifestyle, but he was full of pride and self-righteousness.

Jesus also exposed the Pharisees by pointing out that they made schemes to justify breaking the intent of the Ten Commandments. For instance, He showed that they disobeyed the command to honor their parents through a scheme known as Corban. They would set aside money for religious purposes, then use that money for themselves. At the same time they would make excuses that they had no money to take care of their parents.

The moralist concocts all kinds of schemes to rationalize his behavior. Jesus words, "Do not judge lest you be judged *your-selves.* . . . And why do you look at the speck in your brother's eye, but do not notice the log that is in your own eye?" also expose the moralist. So the moralist is without excuse, for he cannot live up to the things that he teaches.

Moralists Are Unrepentant

Secondly, the moralist is without excuse because of his stubborn unrepentance. In verses 4 and 5 of Romans 2, Paul says that the moralist is unrepentant because he sees no need to repent. He is happy with his lifestyle. Everything seems to be going just fine. If anyone talks to him about his need for salvation, he generally has no awareness of that need in his life. There's no imminent judgment upon him; there's no impending catastrophe that would force him to go deeper into his insufficient resources. So he senses no need in his life for the Gospel of Jesus Christ. He has a hardness of heart that is very difficult to penetrate. The word that Paul uses for stubbornness in verse 5 is the one from which we get our word "sclerosis." Thus arteriosclerosis is hardening of the arteries. Here Paul means the hardening of the heart and spirit that takes place with every act of disobedience even in the life of the moralist.

But the moralist responds, "God is kind, forbearing, and patient. He won't condemn me." When we talk to moral people about Christ, they often say, "Well, look at me. I'm certainly as good as those hypocrites down at the church who say that they are Christians. God is kind and loving. He will accept the good things that I do." Thus he senses no need for repentance. Indeed, he misunderstands the truce that God at this particular time has called with regard to the judgment of sin.

But Paul waves a red flag in front of the moralist and says, "Listen, you've missed the point. The reason God is now patient and longsuffering with regard to your sin is that He wants you to come to repentance." Paul warns that by refusing to repent and respond to God's redemptive love, the moralist is making deposits. He is storing up for himself things that will be used against him on that day when God's truce with unrighteousness ends and His wrath begins to be revealed.

But this judgment is in the future. Since the moralist lives in the present, he has no understanding of the jeopardy into which his unrepentance places his eternal spirit. And as he continues to abuse the patience of God, his own heart becomes harder and harder.

Principles of Divine Judgment

Paul moves to the next step of his argument by presenting the way God views mankind. We should be thankful that the Bible reveals God's criteria of judgment to us. If it did not, we would never know how God looks at us. Because of God's revelation in the Bible, we are not in the dark about the principles God will use to make His decisions in the final judgment. Since we know, we can obey. As Paul sets forth these principles of divine judgment, he also emphasizes other faults of the moralist.

The first principle of divine judgment that Paul presents is performance (Rom. 2:6). He elaborates on this in verse seven by speaking of those who persevere in good deeds out of a proper motivation. Paul shows that God is interested not only in what we profess with the mouth but also in what we do with out lives. Paul agrees with the Apostle James that faith without works is dead. We wrestle with these verses because Paul also teaches that we are not saved by works. We are saved by grace through faith — a gift of God based upon the work of Jesus Christ on our behalf.

But here Paul is speaking of those who have the proper motivation for doing good works. He is not speaking of people who do good works in order to make points with God — those who think they will stand before God on the day of judgment and say, "God, you can't condemn me, because I did so many good deeds." Instead he is talking about those who honestly seek the Lord.

Paul is recommending to the moralist that he respond to God by likewise diligently seeking Him. He is calling upon the moralist to use all of the good things in his life to lead him to God. Perhaps he lives in a place where he has never heard the Gospel of Jesus Christ. Nevertheless he should persevere in doing good and in seeking glory, honor, and immortality. By doing so, he will come to know the Lord (cf. Jer. 29:13).

Therefore, good works, if they are evidence of a desire to know God, can ultimately lead to eternal life. God will make sure that the person who has a desire to know Him will have an opportunity to hear and respond to the gospel.

We have an excellent illustration of this in Acts 10 in the life of Cornelius, the Roman soldier. Cornelius was a good man, a very moral person. He is described as "a devout man, and one who feared God with all his household, and gave many alms to the *Jewish* people, and prayed to God continually" (Acts 10:2).

Cornelius was a good man, but he wasn't a Christian. He was a moralist, but he wasn't saved. Nevertheless, he was doing the right things that could result in his salvation because he was seeking God with all of his life. When we seek God that way, God responds to us. And that's exactly what happened to Cornelius. He received a vision in which he was instructed to make contact with the Apostle Peter, who would come and share the gospel with him and his household.

Notice how the soldiers of Cornelius describe their commander to Peter. They portray him as "a righteous and God-fearing man well spoken of by the entire nation of the Jews" (Acts 10:22). Even his soldiers recognized the high morality of Cornelius.

Notice also what happens when Peter finally arrives on the scene. Cornelius explains to Peter, "And so I sent to you immediately, and you have been kind enough to come. Now then, we are all here present before God to hear all that you have been commanded by the Lord" (10:33). Hearing this Peter replied, "I most certainly understand *now* that God is not one to show partiality, but in every nation the man who fears Him and does what is right, is welcome to Him" (10:34-35).

Cornelius was a properly motivated moralist. He was not

using his good works to justify himself before God. Instead, his morality was motivated by his intense desire to know God fully. The proof of this is in the way he responded when he heard the gospel message.

If his heart is right and if his motivation is proper, the moralist will not let his morality stand between him and God. He will readily recognize his need for Christ and say yes to life eternal. But if a person hears the gospel and comes up with arguments about how good and moral he is and contrasts himself with all of the bad Christian examples he knows, then the motivation for his good works has been selfish ambition, and he will say no to eternal life.

God's Judgment Is Impartial

Paul's next point is that God is impartial (Rom. 2:11-15). God does not evaluate people on the basis of their goodness or their position. He evaluates them on the basis of how they are responding to what they know. How are they responding to the revelation they have received, whatever the level of that revelation? Here Paul mentions the two basic kinds of revelation that have been given. One is the moral law that was given to the Jews. The Jews are held responsible for themselves and their activities on the basis of that law because that is the revelation they received. If they do not obey the law, they are judged by that law itself.

But how will God judge the Gentile moralist? Will God judge that person on the basis of something that he has never heard? No, God will judge that person on the basis of what Paul calls the conscience — the law written on the heart of every human being. As a part of creating us in His own image (though that image is marred and in the bondage of sin), God has placed within every person a witness to Himself. The Bible calls that witness the conscience. Paul says that those who do not have the law still have the conscience.

The word conscience means "to understand with." Therefore the conscience within us has the ability to look at things the way God looks at them. But there is a problem. It is the same problem that was described in Romans 1:18-32. Just as people suppress the revelation of God, even so do they suppress the conscience.

The unbeliever has the voice of conscience in his life. If he would listen to that voice, it would lead him to Jesus Christ.

But he does not listen to the voice God has placed in his life.
Instead, he suppresses his conscience. He goes against it. He
disobeys it. After he has done that for so long, the voice becomes weaker. It becomes softer each time it is violated.

We have seen, then, that God judges on the basis of the law
those who have heard the law. And he judges on the basis of
the conscience those who have not heard the law. But the end
result is the same. Man in his sin suppresses the truth and is
therefore without excuse.

God Judges According to Reality

The third way that God judges is on the basis of reality
(Rom. 2:16). Paul referred to this in Romans 2:2. God judges
according to the truth. God judges rightly. God judges according to reality. God is able to make the distinction between
that which appears to be real and that which is genuinely
real. Humans look on the outward appearance, but God looks
on the heart. He judges on the basis of what He sees happening in the heart of the individual.

Now that works both ways. It can be either good or bad. The
moralist, though he professed a lot of good things, was rotten
in the secrets of his heart. Behind the scenes he tried to see
what he could get away with. God knows this and will judge
that person according to the secrets of the heart.

On the other hand, things are not always what they appear
to be. A young man worked for a rather large company in
New York City. Every Thanksgiving the boss gave a 14 to 16-
pound turkey to each of his employees. Since this young man
was single, he always said that he didn't want the turkey
since he had no use for it.

After several years this became an affront to the boss. So
the other workers said to the young man, "You've got to take
the turkey." Having prepared him this way, the man's friends
thought they would play a practical joke on him. So they
made up a fake turkey of papier-mâché weighing 16 pounds
and appropriately wrapped. When the boss handed out the
turkeys, this young man was given the phony one.

As the man rode home on the subway, he thought, "I don't
have any use for this turkey. What am I going to do with a 16-
pound turkey?" On the subway he saw a poor family. Obviously they were not going to have a very fancy Thanksgiving
dinner. In a genuine spirit of generosity he gave his wrapped

turkey to them, saying, "Happy Thanksgiving."

What do you suppose that family thought when they arrived home, unwrapped the turkey, and discovered it was a fake? The man's motivation in giving it was entirely noble. But the result wasn't very noble. When he went back to work after Thanksgiving and learned what his friends had done, he was heartsick. But there was nothing he could do. He had no way to contact the family, and in the millions of people in New York City, he would probably never see them again.

God examines the secrets of the heart. He sees into our motives. If we play the proper religious game out of improper motives, hoping to get through on pretense, and never make a heart response to Jesus Christ, God knows. But sometimes we are unjustly criticized by others because they do not understand our true motives. Sometimes they read their own unworthy motives into ours. In such cases we don't need to be defensive. We need to understand that God knows the secrets of the heart and that He judges according to what is reality rather than according to what appears to be reality.

So what about the moralist? Does the moralist need to know the gospel, which is the power of God unto salvation? The Apostle Paul says, "Absolutely!" Notice that he began this section saying, "You are without excuse" (Rom. 2:1). Even the moralist, with his honorable lifestyle, is guilty before God. He is defenseless before God because his life is not consistent. Further, it is impossible for him to become consistent. He doesn't even respond positively to what he knows. Indeed, it is impossible for him to do so. He needs the light of the Gospel of Jesus Christ in his life.

We live in a time when it is very easy to say, "Well, that's a very good moral person over there. I really don't need to talk to him about Jesus Christ. Surely God will give him some points for his morality." That is completely contrary to the gospel, which says salvation is a gift. It's not earned by any merit of our own. There must be a heart response to Jesus Christ, even as Cornelius responded when the gospel was presented to him.

QUESTIONS FOR DISCUSSION

1. Who are some prominent non-Christian moralists of our day? In what ways do they manifest the faults that Paul describes?

2. How might you answer a person of good morality who says, "I don't need Christ for I'm just as good as the people in your church."
3. What would you say to a non-Christian moralist who points to the blessings in his life as evidence that God has accepted him on the basis of his good works?
4. How were the good works that Cornelius did different from the good works of the moralist?
5. Why must judgment be left in the hands of God?

CHAPTER FOUR

WHAT ABOUT
THE RELIGIONIST?

Romans 2:17—3:8

A S you recall, in this first section of Romans the Apostle Paul is demonstrating from several perspectives that all people need Jesus Christ. This means *all*, without exception. So far he has considered two categories of people. First he looked at the Gentile world in its depravity. He followed that with his case against the moralist, be he Gentile or Jew. The Apostle Paul showed that the moralist is inconsistent. He cannot live up to his own moral standards, even though he has a revelation of God in his own conscience. The moralist often violates his conscience, and everytime he does, he demonstrates that he needs a savior.

Now in Romans 2:17—3:8, Paul begins to address the Jew. The Jew of Paul's day was a religionist. In contemporary terms, where Paul uses the term Jew, we could substitute any person who is depending upon religion, rather than upon Jesus Christ, for salvation. So we could substitute the Mormon, the Hindu, the Christian Scientist, the Catholic, the Baptist, the Prebyterian, or the Brethren who is depending upon his religion to save him instead of trusting in Jesus and Jesus alone for salvation. A person can be a member of a church and not be a member of the Kingdom of God if he has never received Christ as Savior and Lord. Here Paul addresses this kind of person, the one who is trusting in religion.

In addressing the Jewish religionist, the Apostle Paul begins by saying that the Jews have been given the law of God.

They rely upon it. The law of God has become the foundation for their standing with God. Through the law they know God's will. But they have a problem. They are not able to live according to the law of God which has been given to them. As a result, they are inconsistent. They are not able to live by their own law.

Differences Between Religion and Salvation

We, too, become caught up in inconsistencies when we confuse religion and salvation. The two are not the same. Let's differentiate between the characteristics of religion and the characteristics of salvation.

First, there is a radical difference between the two with regard to their origin. Religion has its source in man. Salvation, on the other hand, has its source in God. They have two different beginning points: religion in man, salvation in God.

But the Jew could say, "Now wait a minute. My religion comes from God. It was God's covenant that was given unto us. It was divine revelation that we received." That is absolutely right. But we learn from reading the New Testament and Jewish history that Jews ritualized the revelation God gave them. They made a lot of little petty rules to interpret God's law, and the interpretation of those rules and living by those rules became their religion. Since these rules were man-made, their origin was in man, not in God.

Second, religion and salvation not only differ in their origin, but they also differ radically in their perspective. Religion is man's attempt to reach God. God has placed within man a desire to know Him, to have that God-shaped vacuum in his life filled. Religion is man's attempt to reach out, to strive, to work, to try trial and error, to do whatever it takes to find that which will meet his need. But salvation is God reaching down to man in Jesus Christ. God has given in Jesus Christ that which man can never gain on his own, no matter how diligently he strives. Religion cannot suffice, but God's salvation satisfies.

Third, religion and salvation are different in their basic philosophies. Religion does not recognize human spiritual need with regard to sin and a savior. Religion does not recognize human depravity or spiritual incapacity. But salvation makes these two basic truths the very pivotal part of the Gospel of Jesus Christ. Because of man's spiritual need and incapacitation, he needs a savior. God supplies that savior in Jesus Christ.

Fourth, religion and salvation differ with regard to their content. No matter what religion you look at, you'll find that it is grounded on a system of thought or "truths" that someone has brought together. If you want to be a part of that religion, you adopt that system of truth and you say, "I believe the basic propositions taught by this religion." But salvation is exactly the opposite. It is not so much truth in a system as it is a Person. Jesus said, "I am the way, and the truth, and the life." Jesus personifies truth. Salvation is a response to a Person who is a person of truth rather than primarily a response to a system of thought. It is true that a system of thought has grown out of the Person of Truth. But we must not put the cart before the horse. Salvation starts with God and His revelation of the truth in His Son, Jesus Christ.

Fifth, salvation and religion differ with regard to their intention. The goal of religion is to make man acceptable to himself—so he can live with himself. But salvation deals with whether a person is acceptable to God. Salvation supplies in Jesus Christ what is necessary so that a person can be accepted by God.

Sixth, religion and salvation differ with regard to their dynamic. Religion is idealistic about what man can do, what man can accomplish. It points with great pride to man's achievements. But that dynamic is not sufficient to provide man's salvation. Religion cannot do it. A new dynamic is needed, and that new dynamic comes from the transforming power of God. In the new birth a person receives Christ into his life. At that point the power of Christ, the power of the resurrection of Christ, comes to live in him personally. That's an entirely different dynamic, and it's the only dynamic that is able to save.

Seventh, religion and salvation differ with regard to their tense. Religion puts the emphasis on what you "do" in the present. It's what you do *now* that matters. But with salvation, it's what *has been done* in the past that's important. It was done by Jesus Christ on the cross when He said, "It is finished." The plan of salvation was accomplished. Religion puts the emphasis on "do" and you will live. Salvation says, "No, live in Jesus Christ, and then you will do; then you will perform."

The Jewish people to whom Paul addressed these words were very religious; nevertheless, they were lost. They had the law, but they were not able to live up to the law in either their actions or their thoughts. Some used religion for their personal profit, just as there are shysters today who make thousands of dollars on religion. Paul said, "You who abhor idols, do you rob temples?" (v. 22). There were four Jewish missionaries who went to Rome to take Judaism, their faith, to the Gentiles. A very wealthy Roman lady accepted their religion. They instructed her to give a large gift to the Temple in Jerusalem. So she gave them a significant gift for the Temple, but it never made it to Jerusalem. Instead, it made it into their pockets. This led to the decree that all Jews should be booted out of Rome. The Jews did not live by their own law. That's the problem with the religionist.

In verse 25 Paul continues to illustrate his point by investigating the Jewish practice of circumcision. Circumcision began with the father of the Jewish faith, Abraham. God made a covenant with Abraham promising that through him all of the nations of the world would be blessed, that he would be the father of a great nation, and that salvation would come through this nation to the world. Abraham believed what God said and responded in faith. And it was this faith that God credited to Abraham as righteousness (Gen. 15:6). Abraham was counted as righteous *before* he was circumcised. Circumcision came later (Gen. 17:9-14) as a physical sign of that covenant which Abraham had accepted by faith.

Paul says that the order is very important. Abraham's righteousness came by faith. This was first. Then circumcision was added as the physical symbol. Circumcision was the sign of the covenant. It was not the means to the covenant. But by the time Paul wrote this letter to the Romans, the Jews had lost sight of the importance of the order. Circumcision had become more important to them than the covenant which it represented.

Making Ritual an End in Itself

This is what religionists always do. They take that which is a ritual, that which is a means to an end, and make it an end in itself. In fact, one of the Jewish rabbis in one of his writings pictured Abraham at the gates of hell refusing to let any circumcised person in. The Jews thought it was impossible for physically circumcised persons to end up in hell. Paul says, "Your circumcision is fine" (v. 25), but he adds a condition. Circumcision is fine if you practice the law. Circumcision is external, but the heart of the matter in Christianity is internal. The act of faith in response to Christ as Savior and Lord is a spiritual matter which must precede the physical sign. But the Jews had turned it around. They were emphasizing the physical sign and ignoring the spiritual.

Who is a Jew? I understand this is a question that's widely debated in the nation of Israel today. They cannot decide on a definition of a Jew. Is being a Jew a matter of culture — for example, keeping a kosher kitchen and observing other Jewish cultural practices? Or is being a Jew a matter of religion — obeying the Torah, accepting the Old Testament scriptures, and worshiping in the synagogue? But an atheist can also be considered a Jew if he is a citizen of the nation of Israel. And for some people, a Jew is a person who has a certain complexion and facial features. Who is a Jew?

Paul identifies the true Jew as the person who has accepted Jesus Christ as his personal Savior. In verse 28 Paul says outward circumcision, physical circumcision, does not make one a Jew. Rather, the true Jew is the person who has had the inner circumcision of the heart through the operation of the Holy Spirit. In God's economy, spiritual circumcision is essential. The human heart must be purified, and no mere physical ritual can accomplish this. The person with the circumcised heart will love the Lord with all his heart and with all his soul. Spiritual life comes from a spiritual, not a physical, source (Deut. 30:6).

Several years ago I spent some time with an organization that sent us out to walk the streets, knock on doors, and talk to people. One of the things we would often ask these people was, "Have you made the wonderful discovery of knowing Jesus Christ personally?" Some people would say, "Oh, I was baptized." Others would say, "Oh, I'm a member of so and so church." Still others would say, "I'm a Catholic," or "I'm a Presbyterian," or whatever. To that kind of response we would say, "That's fine, but have you made the wonderful discovery of knowing Jesus Christ personally in your heart, in your life?"

People's responses show that the flaw of the religionist is still very much with us, namely that the external is more important than the internal. Many people believe that if their name is on the membership list of some church, they are OK — whether or not they ever attend services or live the Christian life. They've taken the external and made it more important than the internal, the spiritual. I've seen it happen many, many times in my ministry, and it always baffles me. Some people respond to Jesus Christ and are baptized, then we never see them again. They go through the external rite — they're baptized — and then it's as if they think, "That's it; I've met the external qualifications; I'm in. What I do with my life from here on out doesn't matter. I don't have to be loyal to Jesus Christ or to His church. I don't have to bear the name of Christ." They put their faith in the physical and external rather than in the spiritual inward response of the heart.

That was the error of the ritualistic Jews. They made that which was merely a physical symbol the reality. The religionist puts a false emphasis on the externals while ignoring the basic thing — the condition of the heart.

Objections of the Religionist

As Paul begins chapter three, he invisions an objector to his statements. When Paul preached in the Jewish synagogues, he often encountered such objectors. So he sees one of these in his mind's eye asking, "Well then, what good is there in being a Jew? What good is there in being circumcised?" (cf. Rom. 3:1).

Similar objections are raised today when we try to make the distinction between external and internal. Instead of coming to a balanced position, people flop over to the other side and say, "Well then, why be baptized at all? Why be circumcised at all? Why do any of the externals? What advantage is there in these?" So this objector asks, "Then what advantage has the Jew? Or what is the benefit of circumcision?"

Paul answers, "You have a great advantage. You were entrusted with the oracles of God. God's word was revealed to you, and that makes you distinct. You do have an advantage, but you have misused that advantage by making the external more important than the internal."

The next objection comes in verse 3. The Jews felt that since God had made a covenant with Abraham and his descendants, they were acceptable to God no matter what they did. They reasoned that since God had made this covenant, if

He went back on it, it was because some Jews had become unfaithful and therefore God would also be unfaithful. They were trying to argue that if some people didn't keep the covenant, not only were they unfaithful, but God was unfaithful as well. The Apostle Paul shoots down this excuse in verse 4 by declaring that God is not unfaithful. God will keep His covenant. In chapters 9, 10, and 11 of Romans, Paul explains how God will fulfill His covenant through the remnant of Jews who remain faithful.

We raise the same kind of objections sometimes, don't we? Here's a person traveling off in unbelief. His life goes down the drain, and we want to blame God. We may say, "God wasn't good. God didn't keep His covenant to that particular person." The Apostle Paul says, "God will always be faithful."

The next objection of this hypothetical questioner is stated in verse 5. Here the questioner tries to justify sin by saying that if people do unrighteous things, this will bring glory to God because it will reveal the righteousness of God. But even *saying* this makes it ludicrous. And yet that was one of the objections some were making. They were saying, in essence, sin will glorify God because it will show the righteousness of God. But Paul goes on to demonstrate that if that were indeed true, God would never be able to judge sin, and justice would be paralyzed. The justice of God would be lost.

The next objection is stated in verses 7 and 8. Paul preached a gospel of justification by grace through faith in Jesus Christ. Some responded by saying, "Good, if God is so gracious and He covers all sin by His grace, then let's sin that we might have more grace." Paul responds, "Such an argument is so faulty, it doesn't even deserve an answer. Their condemnation is just."

But these are the kinds of arguments that religious people make to excuse the fact that they have put the emphasis on the externals rather than on the internals and accept Christ as Savior and Lord. They want to make these rationalizations to prove that there's something wrong with God and His working with man.

Tests for Excuses

This objector in Romans was neither the first nor the last to use an excuse to miss the point about what God wanted him to do with his life. R.A. Torrey, an evangelist and Bible teacher of a bygone generation, had a sermon entitled "The Refuge of Lies," which dealt with excuse-making. He submits four tests to use in scrutinizing excuses to ascertain their validity.

First, does this excuse meet the highest demands of my own conscience? If I make excuses in order to justify and rationalize not walking in God's will, my excuses will not satisfy even my own conscience.

Second, does this excuse make me a better person than I would be if I accepted Christ as my personal Savior? If so, go to it.

Third, will this excuse stand in the hour of death? When I come to my deathbed, things will become very serious. Many of the things I made excuses about all of my life will become much clearer. Will my excuses, which emphasize the externals and ignore the internals, stand in the hour of death?

Fourth, will this excuse stand the test of God's judgment itself? When God, who knows all my secrets and judges me by the secrets of my heart, casts His holy gaze upon my life, will my excuses stand? Or will they crumble like sand castles? The religionist, rather than accepting Christ, emphasizes the external and makes excuses. But these excuses will not pass the judgment.

Where is Paul going with this? Look at verse 9. With this verse he begins the conclusion of the argument of the first part of Romans, namely, that the heathen, the pagan, the perverse, the moral person, the religionist, all have a need. They all need the Gospel of Jesus Christ because it is the power of God unto salvation. Idolatry, morality, religion — they cannot help us. Only salvation in Jesus Christ is sufficient when we stand before God.

QUESTIONS FOR DISCUSSION

1. Are we ever in danger (individually and corporately in the church) of making our Christian faith into a "religion"? If so, in what ways?
2. How does your own faith measure up? Are you putting your trust in "religion" or in salvation in Jesus Christ?
3. What are some Christian rituals that people make ends in themselves? In what ways do they do this?
4. How might you use the four "tests for excuses" given above in witnessing to non-Christians?

MADE RIGHT
BY GOD'S GRACE

CHAPTER FIVE

JUSTIFIED BY GOD'S GRACE

Romans 3:9-31

A WOMAN was getting ready for church when suddenly she dashed into the living room, gazed at her reflection in the mirror, and said, "I looked just awful in that bedroom mirror, but I look better in this one!" The difference may have been due to the quality of the glass or the availability of light. Nevertheless, the lady should not have been so concerned about which mirror made her appear better, but about which one actually gave an honest picture.

Mankind's Problem

Verses 9-31 of Romans chapter three are pivotal in the development of the theological progression of this epistle. In this passage Paul moves from one major section to another. In verses 9-20 he concludes the theme he began in 1:18. After looking at the pagan, the moralist, and the religionist in Romans 1:18—3:8, Paul concludes that all people are sinners. Then in 3:9-20 he puts the clincher on his presentation by quoting an impressive series of six Old Testament scriptures.

As human beings look into the mirror of Scripture, they see a reflection of their true condition outside of Jesus Christ. All without exception — be they pagan, moralist, or religionist — are sinners. As Psalm 14:1 declared (quoted in 3:10), "There is none righteous, not even one." Looking into a different mirror may give a more pleasant picture, but we see the true picture of the human condition both individually and collectively only when we look into the mirror of Scripture.

As Paul holds up that biblical mirror, he quotes five passages from the Psalms (14:1-3; 5:9; 140:3; 10:7; 36:1) and one from Isaiah (59:7-8). Paul's conclusion about the condition of the human race is supported by the authority of God's word. Looking into this mirror, we see a picture of the character of man as God sees it (vv. 10-12). Next we have a description of the kind of conduct which the sinful character of man produces (vv. 13-17). And the final quotation (v. 18) presents the cause of both the sinful character and the sinful conduct.

By means of these Old Testament quotations, Paul demonstrates both the universality of sin in the human race and the inroads sin has made into every facet of individual and corporate life. In this respect the ground at the foot of the cross is level. In this respect the moralist or the religionist is no better than the pagan. All have the same problem. All have turned away from God (v. 12) and as a result have become useless. They no longer seek for a relationship with God. Self-fulfillment has become more important than putting God first in their lives. They devote all their energies to pursuits which seem right but which do not lead to any understanding of God's will and ways. Therefore, in the long run these pursuits have no value. They are both worthless and destructive.

Sinful character expresses itself in sinful conduct, and verses 13-17 show the ramifications of sin in human life. Sin has an all-consuming effect on the sinner because it corrupts his entire being. Notice all the members of the body which are affected: the throat, the tongue, the lips (v. 13), and the mouth (v. 14). Certainly the sinner reveals himself by the way he talks. Jesus said, ". . . the mouth speaks out of that which fills the heart" (Matt. 12:34). Open graves are full of decay. Quite often the spiritual and moral decay caused by sin is clearly revealed not only by one's words but also by one's tone of voice. The destruction worked by the tongue is as deadly as the venom of a poisonous snake.

Other body parts, the feet (v. 15) and eyes (v. 18), are also used to convey the total control sin has over human conduct. The feet of the ungodly are constantly on the warpath, resulting in misery and destruction. Seldom do they travel the paths of peace. They are eager to do wrong and swift to shed blood. The list demonstrates that man's "entire being is adversely affected by sin. His whole nature is permeated with it."[1]

Verse 18 presents the cause of man's perverse character and conduct — he has no reverence for God. His actions are the result of a personality devoid of God, even if that void is camouflaged by an intricate self-righteousness. Reverence means recognizing the proper place for God in one's life. When God is not number one, a person's character is warped and that person's conduct demonstrates that this is the case.

The Role of the Law

What is the role of the law in all of this (vv. 19-20)? Since Paul uses the term "law" here following a list of quotes, none of which came from the "law" section of the Old Testament, he is using the term in a broad sense to refer to the entire Old Testament revelation. The law makes everyone who hears it accountable to God. Because God has revealed in the moral law what is sin and what is righteousness, those who have heard the law can no longer plead ignorance. Human beings are moral creatures, and as such must be held accountable. Accountability necessitates an objective moral standard against which everything is measured. God's word is that standard. When people honestly evaluate themselves by God's moral standard, they have no defense or excuse. Every mouth is silenced.

Unfortunately, many people respond by trying to attack the standard. A Hindu, having seen through a microscope that the "sacred water" of the Ganges River in India was full of filth and disease-causing germs, smashed the instrument to pieces. He could not stand having the error of his beliefs exposed. In the same way, some people seek to discredit God's word when it exposes their sins. But God's standard will endure forever regardless of man's opinion about it.

The law reveals sin, but it is helpless to take sin away. Paul repeats this point in Romans 5:20; 7:7ff. (cf. Gal. 2:16; 3:11). The law loudly proclaims man's need for salvation but cannot itself meet that need.

God has a solution to this dilemma, however, and with his "but now" of verse 21 Paul begins to explain that solution. But before we move to that solution, let's jump to verse 23, a statement which summarizes in a nutshell all that Paul has written since 1:18. God created human beings both for glory and to reveal His glory. But because of sin, that glory no longer shines. Even at his best, man in his sinful condition

is a long way from the glory God intended him to have.
A man had a small white Highland terrier which he kept
spotlessly clean by frequent baths. One night a winter storm
dropped a fresh blanket of glistening snow. As he gazed out
his window, the man saw a drab-looking dog walking across
the snow. He suddenly recognized it as his dog. It was still as
clean as always, but it appeared dirty in comparison with the
brilliant snow. In the same way, the results of sin upon
human nature are overwhelmingly evident when measured
against God's holiness and brilliant glory. God's glory is the
majesty of His holy person. The great tragedy of sin is that
man was out off from fellowship with the God of glory. Clearly
humanity is in despicable condition and is totally helpless to
change that condition.

So far there has not been much gospel in Romans, but now
Paul begins to share the Good News. Up to this point he has
vividly and systematically shown the true human condition.
Now he opens the door to the only solution — God's provision
for mankind's problem.

God's Provision

If doing righteous deeds cannot save us and put us into a
right relationship with God (Tit. 3:5), how can we be saved? If
all human efforts to save ourselves are doomed to failure, how
then can we be saved? Is the situation completely hopeless?

"But now" (v. 21) is a forceful adversative that Paul uses to
begin his explanation of God's solution to mankind's problem.
God's provision is so awesome that Paul draws upon the language of the law court (justification, v. 24), the slave market
(redemption, v. 24), and the Temple (propitiation, v. 25) to try
to explain it. He speaks of the fullness of God's gracious provision in Christ in terms of acquittal or pardon, liberation, and
atonement.

Of all the New Testament writers, the Apostle Paul presents most completely the doctrine of justification by faith
(primarily in Romans and Galatians, but also see II Cor.
5:14ff.; Eph. 2:1ff.; Phil. 3:4ff.). The major section we now
begin (Rom. 3:21—5:20) is the most extensive presentation of
justification found anywhere in the Bible.

To be justified means to be declared righteous. (The root
words for "justification" and "righteousness" are the same and
occur ten times in verses 21-31). Justification is an integral

part of the gospel of salvation, which reveals the righteousness of God and establishes the basic truth of biblical revelation, i.e., "the just shall live by faith" (Rom. 1:16, 17).

To be justified a person must obtain the righteousness of God. But how can that be done? It cannot be accomplished by any human activity, because all have sinned. It could be accomplished by completely obeying God's moral law, but no human being other than Jesus Christ has done that. So that, too, is futile as a way of justification. How to be just in God's sight has been a human dilemma ever since the first sin, and man has found no satisfactory answer.

But that which is impossible for man is not impossible for God. God through Jesus Christ has done for us what we are totally unable to do for ourselves. Jesus came to this earth, lived a life that pleased the righteous God, and died in our place, taking upon Himself the penalty for our sin. Then He rose from the dead for our justification (Rom. 4:25). All who believe in Jesus Christ (3:22) are considered by God to be righteous. When God looks at a believer, He does not see the person's unrighteousness. Instead He sees the righteousness of Christ, and upon that basis He pardons and accepts believing sinners. At that point the person is justified — set right with God. He is acquitted and pardoned because another person, Jesus Christ, took his sentence.

Justification includes the truth that God sees the sinner in terms of his relation to His Son, with whom He is well pleased (see Phil. 3:8, 9). In this sense justification has to do with position, not with character. Once a person is set right with God and is placed in his new position as a child of God, his character will undergo change so that he grows in ethical righteousness. That process is known as sanctification, which Paul considers in Romans 6–8. God provides restoration of relationship with Himself freely, as a gift. What a person cannot earn, God gives to him as an act of grace (v. 24). "God pronounces a man righteous at the beginning of his course, not at the end of it. If He pronounces him righteous at the beginning of his course, it cannot be on the basis of works which he has not yet done; such justification is, on the contrary, 'an act of God's free grace, wherein he pardoneth all our sins, and accepteth us as righteous in his sight' (Westminster Shorter Catechism)."[2]

The second word picture Paul uses in this passage is redemption (v. 24). Redemption took place when a slave was purchased by a new master who intended to set him free from his bondage. It is also the Old Testament picture of Israel's release from the bondage of Egypt (Ex. 15:13; Ps. 77:15; 78:35). According to Ephesians 1:7, the benefit which redemption brings in this life is forgiveness of sins. In the future shall come the redemption of the body (Rom. 8:23), which will complete our salvation.

Propitiation

The third picture Paul uses to give us another perspective on God's saving work comes from the Temple. Propitiation (v. 25) is the same word which the Greek Old Testament used to refer to the "Mercy Seat" on the Ark of the Covenant, which was kept in the Holy of Holies of the Tabernacle (Ex. 25:17; Lev. 16:2, 14-17; cf. Heb. 9:5). As the high priest sprinkled an animal's blood on the Mercy Seat, atonement was made for the sins of the people. Atonement, therefore, has the idea of covering. The blood covered the sins of the people. This was an Old Testament prophecy which was fulfilled by Jesus Christ when He died on the cross, shedding His blood to make atonement for (to cover) our sins. The death of Jesus was a fulfillment of the Old Testament law (3:31).

When the Old Testament High Priest sprinkled the blood on the Day of Atonement, no one else saw him do it, because God had commanded that no one else should be in the Tabernacle (Lev. 16:17). But Jesus was "displayed publicly" (3:25) when He made the ultimate atoning sacrifice by His death on the cross. T.W. Manson says, ". . . the mercy-seat is no longer kept in the sacred seclusion of the most holy place: it is brought out into the midst of the rough and tumble of the world and set up before the eyes of hostile, contemptuous, or indifferent crowds." And Harrison comments, "Indeed, Christ has become the meeting place of God and man where the mercy of God is available because of the sacrifice of the Son."[3]

Propitiation also carried the idea of appeasement of wrath. As the first section of Romans made quite clear, God's response to the unrighteousness of man is wrath (1:18; 2:5, 8; 3:5). Therefore, in order for sinful man to have a relationship with God, God's wrath must be placated. The propitiatory death of Jesus Christ solved the problem of how a holy and righteous God could remain just and at the same time justify sinners. God did not always punish every sin, because His "forbearance" of "sins previously committed" (v. 25) was based on the fact that His righteousness would one day be satisfied (v. 26). God is a God of justice, and justice must be satisfied. Suppose that a man in your town was arrested for murdering 25 children. At the end of the trial, in spite of conclusive evidence of the man's guilt, the judge, wanting to be a nice guy, acquitted him. You can imagine the howls of protest that decision would cause. Why? Because justice was not satisfied. In a similar way, God could not remain righteous if He just winked at man's sin. His justice has to be satisfied. But what could man possibly offer to appease God's justice? Man of himself has nothing sufficient to offer. Therefore God in His love stepped in. He Himself provided the only sacrifice that could satisfy His justice. Read Romans 5:8 to see how God demonstrated His love.

Because of the sacrifice of Jesus Christ on the cross as a lamb without blemish and without spot (I Pet. 1:19), God can both maintain His justice and also enter into relationship with (justify) sinful human beings. Thus, the cross of Jesus Christ is the statement *par excellence* about both the wrath of God and the love of God. "In the self-offering of Christ, God's own righteousness is vindicated and the believing sinner is justified. For Christ occupies a unique position as God's representative with man and man's representative with God. As the representative Man He absorbs the judgment incurred by human sin; as the representative of God he conveys God's pardoning grace to men."[4] God in His grace provided the solution for the problem mankind could not solve.

Experiencing God's Provision

Having explained the intricacies of God's provision through justification, redemption, and propitiation, Paul turns his attention in verses 27-31 to explaining how a person can experience God's provision. Since our salvation is a result of God's work on our behalf, no one can boast that he has achieved salvation. The boastful, self-righteous person has no understanding of God's grace (Eph. 2:8, 9). A gift (v. 24) can never be earned. All a person can do is receive it by faith. Through faith one becomes a beneficiary of what God has done in Jesus Christ.

Paul mentions faith nine times in this pivotal section (vv. 21-31). The only legitimate and efficacious object of faith is Jesus Christ (vv. 22, 26) and His blood (v. 25). Faith is a law in the sense that God has ordained it as the only condition for receiving salvation. Faith is simply the hand of the heart that reaches out to receive what God bestows. Faith is not a work in the sense that one earns salvation by exercising it. Instead faith appropriates what God has done. Since salvation is the work of God and not the work of man, human boasting is excluded. If any boasting is done, God's salvation should be its content (I Cor. 1:30, 31).

Justification by faith removes all human imposed distinctions (vv. 22, 29-30) and makes salvation available to both Jew and Gentile alike (cf. Rom. 9:30-32). In fact, as the writer of Hebrews also asserts (Heb. 11), faith alone pleases God and appropriates His promises. The ground at the foot of the cross is level in this regard as well. The way of salvation is appropriated by all those who believe, whether Jew or Gentile. The saving work of Jesus Christ fulfilled the law and forever installed faith as God's *modus operandi*.

Paul proceeds in the next chapter to use two Old Testament personalities to demonstrate that the law of faith truly established God's intentions in giving the law. God's provision — justification — available through faith alone is the heart of God's way of saving all kinds of people throughout all of human history. In this powerful paragraph, we have the core of the gospel according to Paul. His subsequent chapters illustrate it and explore its various ramifications.

QUESTIONS FOR DISCUSSION

1. In what respects are the moralist and the religionist no better than the pagan? In what respects might they be worse?
2. How do the various parts of the human body (eyes, tongue, hands, feet, etc.) reveal the total control sin has over human conduct (of the unsaved)?
3. To what extent do you think that modern-day attacks on the authority of the Bible are rooted in man's rebellion against God's moral standard?
4. What particular facet (or facets) of God's provision for our salvation is brought out by each of the three words developed in this chapter — justification, redemption, and propitiation?
5. According to Paul, what is the core of the gospel?

CHAPTER SIX

JUSTIFICATION BY FAITH ILLUSTRATED

Romans 4:1-25

IN chapter four of Romans the Apostle Paul begins to elaborate on the essentials of the gospel which he has just presented in chapter three. This is that powerful gospel which Paul had preached so often and which had transformed multitudes of lives and brought about the establishment of many churches. It was good news then and is still good news today.

Paul began his presentation of the gospel by demonstrating that every person needs a savior. All have sinned and fallen short of the glory of God. Therefore all human beings, regardless of their position or category, need a savior. Having established the need for a savior, Paul went on to present the gospel, which proclaims that God has met this need through justification by grace through faith. The Good News is that people can come into a right standing with God by believing in the effectual work of Jesus Christ on the cross.

In lesson five we began to explore the astonishing topic of justification, as we considered the transition passage which took us from the depressing reality of man's need through the open door of God's provision. We learned that we are justified as a gift of God's grace through the redemption which is in Christ Jesus. The undergirding of justification by faith is the atoning ministry of Jesus Christ through His death on the cross. He gave Himself as a sacrifice to redeem us from the slavery of sin, to satisfy the justice of God, and to express God's love for us.

After giving us in Romans 3:21-31 the basics of how we are set right with God through faith, Paul uses all of chapter four to illustrate this great truth. The illustration he uses is Abraham. Abraham was an Old Testament man of faith who was set right with God because he believed God, and God counted that belief unto him for righteousness.

As Paul presents this illustration, he deals with three possible ways by which people have sought to attain right standing with God. He demonstrates that each of these ways is inadequate. Some people seek to become right with God through their good works. Others think that they can become right with God through performing external rites and ordinances. Others think that they can become right with God by obeying the law. Paul not only declares that each of these ways is inadequate, but he also explains why. Then he concludes the chapter by pinpointing the nature of Abraham's faith, saying that what was written about Abraham was written for our good. The principle that was active for the righteousness of Abraham is the very same principle that is active for us today. Justification by grace through faith is not a new concept. It clearly goes back at least 4,000 years to Abraham.

Abraham Was Not Justified by Works

In Romans 4:1-8 Paul declares that Abraham was justified by faith, not by works. He demonstrates that good works are not a means by which we can come into right standing with God. Such a statement about Abraham was shocking to the Jews. They believed that Abraham attained righteousness by his many good works. And to be sure, if it were possible for anyone to work his way into a right relationship with God, certainly Abraham was that person. Even God commended Abraham's righteous deeds, saying to him: "And I will multiply your descendants as the stars of heaven, and will give your descendants all these lands; and by your descendants all the nations of the earth shall be blessed; because Abraham obeyed Me and kept My charge, My commandments, My statutes and My laws (Gen. 26:4-5). In these verses, God, in reaffirming the promise He made earlier to Abraham (Gen. 12:1-3; 15:5), is commending Abraham for his tremendous obedience in the case of his son, Isaac (Gen. 22:1-18). But Abraham's works were not an attempt to earn righteousness. They were an expression of righteousness he had already attained by faith (Gen. 15:6).

Abraham was called the friend of God. He is also the father of the three monotheistic religions of the world. He is the father of the Jews. He is likewise acknowledged as Father Abraham by Moslems, who trace their belief in one God to him. And he is also the spiritual father of all Christians (Gal. 3:29). Yet even a man this great was not set right with God by the great and outstanding things that he did. How was he set right with God? Romans 4:3 gives the answer succinctly: "And Abraham believed God, and it was reckoned to him as righteousness."

Back in Genesis 12 and 15, God made Abraham a promise that many descendants would come from him, that these descendants would possess a land that He would give them, and that through Abraham all nations of the earth would be blessed. The problem was that Abraham had no offspring through whom this promise could be realized. He waited many years for that offspring to be born. Finally, "the word of the LORD came to Abram [Abraham] in a vision, saying, 'Do not fear, Abram, I am a shield to you; Your reward shall be very great.' And Abram said, 'O Lord GOD what wilt Thou give me, since I am childless, and the heir of my house is Eliezer of Damascus [his slave]?' And Abram said, 'Since Thou hast given no offspring to me, one born in my house is my heir.'

"Then behold, the word of the LORD came to him, saying, 'This man will not be your heir; but one who shall come forth from your own body, he shall be your heir.' And He took [Abraham] outside and said, 'Now look toward the heavens, and count the stars, if you are able to count them.' And He said to him, 'So shall your descendants be' " (Gen. 15:1-5).

Abraham Believed God

Now what was Abraham's response to this promise? Genesis 15:6 says, "Then he believed in the LORD; and He reckoned it to him as righteousness." Abraham's right standing with God did not result from meritorious deeds by which he tried to earn acceptance and status with God. No, it came because he believed God. Notice the exact wording of Romans 4:3. It doesn't say that Abraham believed *in* God or that Abraham believed *there is* a God. No, he *believed God.*

Often as we encounter people and talk with them about their relationship with God, their response is, "Oh, I believe

there's a God. I believe there's a Supreme Being out there."
And they have names for Him; for example, "The Man Up-
stairs." They believe that there is somebody who maybe
created the world. They say that they believe in a Supreme
Being. At least they give some kind of intellectual assent to
the idea that there is a Supreme Being.

But this casual, flippant attitude about God's existence is
not the faith the Bible has in mind. Rather the Bible says,
"Abraham believed God." This means that when God made
this verbal promise to Abraham, Abraham believed Him. He
took what God said to him at face value. He believed God. He
then demonstrated his faith by ordering his life according to
what God had promised him. Abraham believed that God was
a God of integrity whose promise could be trusted. Because of
his belief in the fidelity and trustworthiness of God, Abraham
was looked upon by God as righteous. The result was his right
standing with God.

Salvation Is a Gift

Paul goes on to say that righteousness is not of works, because it is a gift that God gives to those who believe Him (vv.
4-5). If we work for our salvation, it isn't a gift. It's something
we earn. When we work, we expect wages in return. Our
paycheck is not a gift. We earned it. The employer owes it to
us. But our standing with God is not earned. We receive it as
a gift (Rom. 3:24). God justifies the ungodly person who places
his faith in Him. As a result, the person's lawless deeds are
forgiven and his sin is covered over. God no longer looks at
the ledger of a person's life and sees the debits of his sins, for
the person's account book has been filled with the righteousness of Christ (vv. 6, 8). This is good news!

If we can be set right with God only through our good
works, everyone is eliminated from the possibility of being
right with God. If we expect to impress a holy, righteous God
with our works, we have to be perfect. We have to meet every
one of God's criteria. We cannot allow the smallest spiritual
detail to slip by in our thoughts or actions, if we expect to
earn our salvation by good works. If we could attain perfec-
tion by our own efforts, God would be obligated to accept us. If
we were perfect, we would not need God's grace. Since no one
is perfect, however, all are excluded from God. But God justifies the ungodly who believe Him and accept the salvation

given in His Son, Jesus Christ (Eph. 2:8, 9).

Abraham was justified by faith, not by works. He demonstrates how people get right with God. He believed God. So must we. There is no other way.

Abraham Was Not Justified by Circumcision

Paul uses the next paragraph (vv. 9-12) to show that Abraham was justified by faith, not by circumcision. Remember that circumcision was the external sign and seal that God gave to Abraham to validate the covenant. In these verses Paul establishes a time sequence. Time is the crux of this argument. When, exactly, was Abraham counted righteous? Was it before his circumcision, or at the time of his circumcision?

In Genesis 15 the promise was given to Abraham that he would have multitudes of descendants. At the time this promise was given, Abraham was not circumcised. Ten years passed and nothing happened. Abraham still had no children. How could he become a great nation? Evidently (and understandably from our point of view) Abraham began to doubt. Maybe he needed to do something. So, with Sarah's help, Abraham concocted a plan to have a child by means of Sarah's handmaiden, Hagar. As a result of this plan, Abraham had a son, Ishmael.

But God's promise would be fulfilled not by human ingenuity, but by divine miracle. Abraham's excursion into impatience created enormous pain and heartache. If Abraham's salvation had been based on works, he would have forfeited it right here. But it wasn't. Thirteen years after Ishmael's birth, God in His grace came to Abraham and reaffirmed His covenant with him. It was not until this point (Gen. 17:1-14) that circumcision was instituted as the external sign and seal of the renewal of the initial covenant of grace (Gen. 15). But Abraham was not first counted righteous at the time of circumcision. No, he was counted righteous from the time of the initial covenant in Genesis 15. Abraham's right standing before God did not result from an external rite. Circumcision merely confirmed in a physical way what he already possessed spiritually (Rom. 4:10, 11).

Thus Paul warns against sacramentalism. People do not come into a right relationship with God simply by participating in the sacraments of the church or by completing a prescribed set of external rituals. For example, some people believe that they receive salvation as a result of their physical baptism. They believe that the means of grace is in this sacrament.

This view was expressed to me several years ago by a man who said that he wanted to be baptized. As we talked, he said, "I hope my baptism will make me a better person and will help me solve the sin problem with which I'm struggling." This man was looking for some inherent power in baptism that would solve all of his problems. But externals don't work that way. The Bible clearly teaches that salvation is a matter of the heart. The power is in the Holy Spirit, who enters our life, not in an external ritual. The crucial factor is not physical circumcision but the spiritual circumcision of the heart. So we, like Abraham, are not set right with God by external rituals. They are important as signs and seals of the faith, but they are not the means by which one is set right with God. We are justified by faith, not by externals.

Abraham Was Not Justified by the Law

In the next paragraph (vv. 13-17) Paul declares that Abraham was justified by faith, not by the law. We are not set right with God by keeping the law. The law makes a promise. It promises that if you live up to its standards, you shall live. If you keep the standard of the law, you will be blessed. But because of our human condition, this is a worthless promise. The other side of the coin is that if you do not keep the standard of the law in its entirety, you will be cursed. Since no human being can fully keep the law, the promise of the law gives us no hope. We are under the curse of the law.

Are you fairly athletic? I will give you $1,000 if you can stand on the ground and jump up and touch the top of the steeple of your church. I have made you a promise. But it is a worthless promise. Why? Because no human being has the ability to do what the promise requires.

So it is with the law. The law is serious business. The law is God's moral standard. But there is no human being who has the ability to keep the law. Jesus summarized the law in love (Matt. 22:36-40). If you can demonstrate in your life 100 percent love toward God and toward others 100 percent of the time, then you can be set right with God by keeping the law. But is there anybody who can do this? If there is, I want to

follow that person around for a few days! No, there is no one
who can do this. Therefore, it is impossible for anyone to be
set right with God by keeping the law.

So the grace of God enters the picture. The law defines violations and transgressions. The broken law cries out for justice in the form of punishment on the transgressor. But grace,
promise, and faith are God's responses (read Rom. 4:16). God
acted in *grace* when He took the initiative and came to
Abraham. Likewise, God took the initiative of *grace* and came
to us in Jesus Christ. God made a *promise* of many descendants to Abraham, and Abraham's response to that promise of
grace was faith. He took God at His word. Likewise, the gospel proclaims the *promise* of salvation that whosoever believes
in Jesus Christ will receive the gift of eternal life. God in His
grace gives us what we could never earn. We are asked to
make a response of *faith* to receive His gift.

There's an old hymn that says:

> *"Do this and live," The Law demands,*
> *But gives me neither feet nor hands.*
> *A better word is "Grace doth bring."*
> *It bids me fly, but gives me wings.*

The law condemns, but grace enables. Using Abraham as
an illustration, Paul has shown that we are not set right with
God by works (vv. 1-8), by externals (vv. 9-12), or by keeping
the law (vv. 13-17).

Abraham's Faith Anticipated Christian Faith

Paul concludes his illustration by showing that Abraham's
faith was anticipatory of Christian faith (vv. 18-25). As verses
23 and 24 say, "Now not for his sake only was it written . . .
but for our sake also . . . ." We should believe in the God of
Abraham (v. 17). He believed in a God "who gives life to the
dead and calls into being that which does not exist." The object of Abraham's faith was a God of life, a God of resurrection, a God of creation who has the power to say to nothing,
"Let there be light," and light comes; who has the power to
say to nothing, "Let the earth be formed," and an earth is
formed.

Faith is only as valuable as the object in which it is placed.
The real issue is not how much faith you have, but the nature
of that in which you place your faith. We put faith in our car's

brakes all the time. When we head down a hill, we believe that the brakes will stop us when we apply them. But suppose the brake line bursts. We still have all the faith in the world that the car will stop, but it doesn't. Why? The object of our faith has let us down. Faith is only as valuable as its object.

You may wake up at three in the morning with a bad headache, stumble to the medicine cabinet, and open its door with all kinds of cobwebs over your eyes. Half awake, you reach for a bottle that you think is aspirin, but it's really roach tablets! In all sincerity you take those tablets believing they are aspirin. On your tombstone they write, "He died in faith."

The object of faith is crucial to our understanding of faith. Abraham believed not **what**, but **whom** — God. The only valid faith is one that has God as its object. Abraham believed in a God who could bring life out of death. Death described several aspects of Abraham's circumstance. When God first promised Abraham many descendants, Abraham was 75 years old. Twenty-four years later, nothing had happened. By every understanding of human biology, it was impossible for Abraham to have even one descendant. Being nearly 100 years old, Abraham was as good as dead. And certainly Sarah's womb was dead (v. 19).

Abraham knew all these impossible circumstances, but he did not waver in unbelief (v. 20). In fact, Paul says he grew strong in faith (v. 20). During 24 years of waiting for the promise to be fulfilled, Abraham didn't vacillate. Instead his faith stayed alive and dynamic, and he gave glory to God, praising Him all the time. How could he do this? Because Abraham knew that balanced against all these insurmountable conditions was the promise of God: "I'm going to make a great nation out of you, Abraham, and it will not come out of your slave's house. It will come from your own body." How did Abraham respond to that promise? He believed that God could bring life out of death! And that's exactly what happened. Isaac was born — the miracle offspring of Abraham and Sarah.

Abraham's faith was effective because it was placed in a powerful God who performs what He promises (v. 21). Likewise, we must put our faith in the God who has the ability to do what He says He will do. Verses 23-25 give the application. Our spiritual birth by our own efforts is as unlikely and impossible as was Sarah's ability to give birth to a child. But God brings life out of spiritual death. He did this through the death and the resurrection of Jesus Christ, and He offers spiritual life out of spiritual death to all mankind. Paul says that every one who believes in Him who raised Jesus our Lord from the dead is counted by God as righteous. The righteousness of Jesus Christ is credited to that person's eternal account and, as a result, that person has right standing with God.

From Abraham we learn that we are not saved by our own efforts. Neither are we saved by performing certain external acts or by diligently striving to keep the law. Instead we are saved by believing in the God who has promised us salvation in Jesus Christ and who has demonstrated the validity of His promise by raising Jesus Christ from the dead. Abraham believed God and received his right standing with God. God has given us a Savior who died for our sins and rose again that we might have right standing with Him. The righteousness of God is not a goal we achieve. It is a gift we receive. Believe God!

QUESTIONS FOR DISCUSSION

1. What is the difference between believing God and believing in God?
2. In addition to baptism, what are some other sacraments or rituals that people trust in for salvation?
3. If we are not saved by our works, what place do works have in our Christian lives?
4. Why is it impossible for a person to be saved by keeping God's law?
5. In what ways is Abraham's faith an example of what Christian faith should be?

CHAPTER SEVEN

THE CORNUCOPIA OF JUSTIFICATION

Romans 5:1-11

IN chapter five Paul continues his development of the great theme of justification by faith, which he began in the previous chapter. Viewing justification as an accomplished fact, he begins to itemize the results of being in a right relationship with God. He takes us on a guided tour of the cornucopia of justification, pointing out some of the specific benefits that belong to those who are in a right relationship with God through faith in Jesus Christ.

Paul begins this chapter with an established fact: "Therefore having been justified by faith . . . (v. 1). This is the foundation upon which all our life with God is constructed. Paul speaks of our justification in the past tense. Earlier in this epistle he described the condition of the world without Christ. Now He enumerates the blessings that belong to those who have accepted Christ.

Peace With God

The first blessing in the cornucopia of justification is peace with God. "Therefore having been justified by faith, we have peace with God through our Lord Jesus Christ" (v. 1). Peace with God means that God looks with favor upon those who respond to Christ as Savior and Lord. Peace with God means being in an amicable relationship with Him.

But note that Paul is writing about peace *with* God, not about the peace *of* God. The peace *of* God is a person's subjec-

65

tive experience of spiritual and emotional serenity. Note also that Paul is not writing about peace of mind. The peace of God and the peace of mind that Christians experience are out-growths of being at peace *with* God through our Lord Jesus Christ. Our relationship with Him has been reestablished. The alienation caused by sin has been dealt with by Christ through His death on the cross. As a result, we can come into a new relationship with God. We can be at peace with Him.

William Barclay tells of an experience Rosita Forbes had one night during her travels in China. She came to a village and could find no place to stay. So she ended up spending the night in one of the Chinese temples filled with their gods. In the middle of the night she awoke. The moon was shining into the temple and she could see the faces of these gods. The facial expression on each one of these idols was a snarl or a sneer. This is the concept of the gods of people who have never heard of Jesus Christ. They instinctively recognize their own inadequacy to stand before God. They believe that God is angry with them. Therefore their gods snarl and sneer at them.

How different the message of Christianity! In Jesus Christ we know God as a God of love. The snarl has become a smile. In Jesus Christ God comes to us with open arms. Jesus made this possible by obliterating the hostility, enmity, and aliena-tion that sin brought to the relationship between people and God. Therefore we have peace with God *through* our Lord Jesus Christ. He *is* our peace (Eph. 2:14). Only through Jesus Christ can sinful man be at peace with the holy God.

Access to God

Verse 2 speaks of one immediate result of this peace: ". . . we have obtained our introduction by faith into this grace in which we stand . . . ." As a result of having peace with God, we also have access to God. We can come directly to God in Jesus Christ. Indeed, He throws open the door of His life to us.

Perhaps one of the best ways to illustrate the access we have in Christ is to remember how it is in countries where there is royalty. Not every Tom, Dick, and Harry can waltz into the palace, dance into the king's throne room, and expect to be welcomed. If a person tries that, armed guards will throw him out. He doesn't have access to the king.

The Old Testament book of Esther illustrates the importance of access and who grants it. This book tells the story of the young Jewish maiden Esther who was taken by Ahasuerus, king of the Medes and the Persians, to be his wife. Through court intrigue and scheming, the evil nobleman Haman secured a royal degree permitting the extermination of the Jews. Esther's uncle, Mordecai, entreated Esther to go to the king to intercede for her people. Esther hesitated at first because even though she was queen, she did not automatically have access to the king. Access was only at his discretion (Est. 4:11). If the king refused access, death was the sentence. Esther knew that if she walked into the king's throne room, *Ahasuerus had the option* of either putting forth his scepter and granting her an audience or of refusing her an audience as an uninvited intruder. Access was at the discretion of the king.

Who are we, as defiled sinners; to think that we should have access to a holy, righteous God? But by a new relationship with God, which He made possible, we are at peace with Him. And He holds forth His scepter to us. He opens the door to us, and we have access to Him.

Not only do we have access, but we have one who introduces us — Jesus Christ, the Son of God. Whenever someone accepts Christ as Savior and Lord, an introduction immediately takes place. The new Christian is announced and welcomed into the throne room of God. Christians have acceptance with God through Jesus Christ, our introducer.

Hope of the Glory of God

The next blessing in the cornucopia of justification is hope (v. 2). In verses 2-5 Paul builds a series of virtues of which hope is both the foundation and the capstone. Hope conditions our response to tribulation; tribulation gives birth to perseverance; perseverance produces character; and character generates additional hope. Each virtue uses the preceding one as a foundation for its development Then it becomes the foundation on which the next virtue is built.

Having been made right with God, we now have the hope of the glory of God. According to Romans 3:23, sin stripped mankind of the glory of God. As sinners we fall short of God's glory. But in justification the hope of the glory of God is restored to us. This hope is not something we create. It's not wishful thinking. It's not some fancy of the imagination. This hope is a noun. It's something that the Christian possesses right now. It is absolutely certain that one day those who are justified by faith in Jesus Christ will again possess the glory of God.

From God's perspective this glory is an accomplished fact. In our experience, however, it is still deferred. Therefore, we both need and have hope. We look forward to that day when we shall be completely made whole, when everything about the sin nature shall be eradicated and we shall be glorified. This hope is one of the results of having been set right with God through faith in Jesus Christ.

Exult in Tribulations

On a practical level this glorious hope makes it possible for us to "exult" even in our tribulations. We live in a world in which Murphy's Law runs rampant. If anything can possibly go wrong, it will. Multitudes of songs have been written about the trials, distresses, problems, and pressures of this life. But Paul declares that as Christians we look at these things from a new perspective — the hope of the glory of God. We can rejoice when pressures come, because God works through them to accomplish His spiritual purpose in our lives and to teach us total dependence on Him. These pressures are not fun to experience, but we can rejoice in the way God works through them to reach His goal of bringing us to maturity in Jesus Christ.

Knowing this we are to persevere through our difficulties. Perseverance is the ability to bear a burden without being broken by its weight. Tribulation not only tests our strength in the Lord, it also increases our strength in the Lord. The weight lifter uses the same principle. He uses the weights to increase his strength. The more he perseveres, the more weight he can lift. He can lift more weight because he is stronger. When tribulation comes to us, we must understand that God is using this test to make us stronger in Him. Therefore, we must persevere. We must not break under the pressure. Since God is our strength, we need not break.

Perseverance has a product — proven character. Job testified to this. He declared, "When He has tried me, I shall come forth as gold" (Job 23:10). The fiery trials burn out the dross and the refined product is proven character (Rom. 5:4). Research departments of corporations use all kinds of apparatus to test their products. Tennis balls are pounded, shot against walls, and squashed by machines to prove their resilience. Tennis ball commercials declare that their ball has been tested and has passed the test. It now has "proven character." God uses the trials of life to manufacture a high-quality person, one who has proved his character by passing through the tests.

The capstone of this process is hope. We are headed toward a realized hope. We begin with hope and we end with hope. A young man was learning to drive an automobile. As the boy tried to maneuver the weaving vehicle, the instructor said, "Son, you'll steer straighter if you look farther down the road!" That is also good spiritual advice. As we move through the tribulations of life, we need to keep the distant hope in view. If our eyes are focused on the hope that will one day be realized, if our eyes are on God's ultimate purposes being fulfilled in our lives, we will steer a straighter course through the adversities of life. We move toward a certain hope, which will not disappoint us.

An Outpouring of God's Love

How do we know that this hope is not a cruel illusion or a figment of our imagination? Our present experience of the outpouring of God's love in our hearts through the Holy Spirit verifies that the future in Christ will not be a disappointment (Rom. 5:5). This verse contains Paul's first use of the word love in this epistle, and he uses it in the subjective sense — to refer to our experience of God's love. At the point of conversion, a Christian is baptized in God's supernatural love, and that love permeates his whole being. As a result we know God's love not only theologically, but also experientially. And just as certainly as we have been flooded with God's love through the Holy Spirit, we shall also obtain the hope promised to us.

In verses 6, 8, and 10 Paul proceeds to proclaim the greatness and the extent of God's love by using the phrase "while we were . . . ." In verse 6 he says, "while we were still helpless"; in verse 8, "while we were yet sinners"; and in verse 10, "while we were enemies."

On our own, outside of Jesus, we are helpless, having no ability to save ourselves. We are sinners — tragic failures who cannot measure up to the glory of God. We are enemies of

God in rebellion against Him. Thus Paul quickly reviews for us the condition of unregenerate mankind. Why? Because he wants to emphasize the magnitude of God's love for us. God does more than merely say to us, "I love you." He goes beyond words to action. He "demonstrates" His love for us by concrete action. He sent His son to die for us. Romans 5:8 is the John 3:16 of the Book of Romans. God's love is both objective and subjective. It is objective in that God sent Jesus Christ into human history to die on the cross for a helpless, rebellious bunch of failures. But we also experience His love subjectively, because He has filled the hearts of believers with His love through the Holy Spirit.

The story is told of an atheist who was standing on a street corner blaspheming God. He finally cried out, "If there is a God in heaven, I challenge Him to strike me dead in five minutes!" Breathless silence reigned as the seconds ticked off. After the five minutes had passed and nothing had happened, this sacrilegious scoffer cried out with a sneer, "You see, there is no God, or by this time He would have struck me dead."

Just as the atheist was about to leave, however, an elderly woman stepped up to him and asked, "Do you have any children?"

"One son," the man replied.

"If your son gave you a knife and told you to kill him, would you do it?" she asked.

"Of course not," the atheist quickly answered.

"Well, why not?" the lady asked.

"Simply because I love him too much!" the athiest replied.

Before turning away, the little lady explained, "It's also because God loves YOU so much, even though you are an atheist, that He refuses to accept your foolish challenge. He wants you saved, not lost."

With these simple words this dear woman gave utterance to the most profound truth of the gospel, as presented here by the Apostle Paul.

Occasionally we hear accounts of human valor, where one person gives his life for another. While these stories are impressive, the love of God is even more impressive. In most instances, one human being dies to save another good person. But God's love went far beyond that. He sent Christ to die for *sinners*. Notice how Paul personalizes it: ". . . while **we** were yet sinners, Christ died for **us**" (v. 8).

And can it be that I should gain
An int'rest in the Savior's blood?
Died He for me, who caused His pain?
For me, who Him to death pursued?
Amazing love! how can it be
That Thou, my God, shouldst die for me?
                    Charles Wesley

Reconciliation

Verses 9-11 give us another result of justification — reconciliation. Reconciliation means that two parties who had been alienated from each other have been brought back into a harmonious relationship. The hostility which separated them has been eradicated and peace has been restored.

Sin caused a separation between God and mankind. Sin created a wall where once a peaceful relationship filled with communication existed. Since mankind was helpless, he could do nothing to restore this relationship. Because of sin, mankind came under the judgment of God. But because of the death of Jesus Christ, we are saved from the wrath of God. As a supreme act of love, Jesus Christ took upon Himself God's wrath against our sins. Thus He brought about reconciliation. "We were reconciled to God *through* the death of His Son" (v. 10). Those who are "saved" (vv. 9, 10) have their relationship with God restored.

Notice Paul's use of "much more" (in verses 9 and 10). Think of what God did for us while we were His enemies. How "much more" will He do now that we are again His friends through reconciliation? "We shall be saved by His life" (v. 10). Christ's work is not only past tense (the cross), but also present tense (Christ lives His life in me — Gal. 2:20). And in the future we shall share the full resurrection life with our glorified Savior! No more complete reconciliation is possible.

No condemnation now I dread;
Jesus, and all in Him, is mine!
Alive in Him, my living Head,
And clothed in righteousness divine,
Bold I approach th' eternal throne,
And claim the crown, through Christ my own.
                    Charles Wesley

What is our response to all these blessings from the cornucopia of justification? Paul says that "we exult in God" (v. 11). We rejoice in God, our Savior. As recipients of these blessings, how could we not rejoice? Paul used the same word in verses 2 and 3; "We exult in hope of the glory of God," and "we also exult in our tribulations." Now he says, let's focus not only on the blessings, let's focus on the one who blesses. Let us "exult in God."

QUESTIONS FOR DISCUSSION

1. What is the difference between peace with God and the peace of God? How are the two related?
2. Why should the Christian's attitude toward the pressures and difficulties of life be different from the non-Christians? In what ways should these attitudes be different?
3. What objective proof do we have that God loves us? What subjective proof?
4. How has reconciliation through Christ changed our relationship to God? How should this affect our attitudes and feelings toward God?
5. How do the truths discussed in this chapter relate to your individual fears, problems, and needs?

CHAPTER EIGHT

THE FIRST AND SECOND ADAMS

Romans 5:12-21

THE few seconds left in the game were rapidly ticking away. The score was 17 to 13, but the team that was behind had advanced the football to the opponents fourteen yard line. Then, using their last time out with five seconds to go, they set up a play to score what would be for them the winning touchdown.

Each player knew his assignment. The outcome of the game was on the line. The center snapped the ball to the quarterback, who faded back and rifled a pinpoint pass to the wide receiver on a crossing pattern. The receiver dove for the ball, making a super catch in the end zone for the winning touchdown just as the gun sounded to end the game!

But the initial thrill of victory turned into the agony of defeat. A penalty flag on the turf loomed bigger than life. An offensive lineman had been caught holding an opposing player. The penalty nullified the score and the game was over. Defeat replaced victory. Elation turned to dejection. The illegal action of one person affected the entire team. One person made the mistake, but the whole team shared the consequences. That's the concept of solidarity.

The Concept of Solidarity

The concept of solidarity is also found in the Bible. In Romans 5:12-21, the Apostle Paul explains how the sin of the first Adam affected the entire human race. He also explains the work of another Adam, the Second Adam (cf. I Cor. 15:20-22; 42-49), and tells how that work affected the human race. Both Adams were representatives of the entire human race. But the decisions and behavior of each had radically different effects on mankind both collectively and individually.

As Paul concludes his major section on the doctrine of justification, he contrasts the consequences of the actions of these two Adams. The sin of the first Adam necessitated the redemptive work of the Second Adam. Each of the two representative Adams heads up a race. The two Adams acted in ways that brought two radically different results.

The following diagram by H.W. Byrne pictures all the contrasts between the two Adams presented in this paragraph.[1]

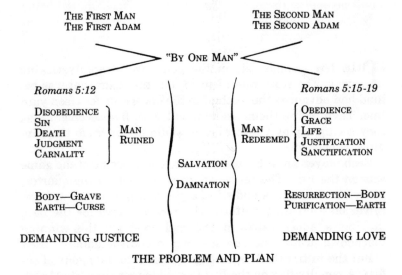

THE FIRST MAN
THE FIRST ADAM

THE SECOND MAN
THE SECOND ADAM

"BY ONE MAN"

Romans 5:12

DISOBEDIENCE
SIN
DEATH
JUDGMENT
CARNALITY
} MAN RUINED

SALVATION

DAMNATION

MAN REDEEMED {

Romans 5:15-19

OBEDIENCE
GRACE
LIFE
JUSTIFICATION
SANCTIFICATION

BODY—GRAVE
EARTH—CURSE

RESURRECTION—BODY
PURIFICATION—EARTH

DEMANDING JUSTICE

DEMANDING LOVE

THE PROBLEM AND PLAN

The disobedience of the first Adam resulted in spiritual death for the race he represented. The obedience of the Second Adam results in deliverance from the death sentence for the race He represented. Both Adams represented the human race. The first enslaved it to spiritual ruination. The second liberated it through spiritual redemption.

To further visualize the contrast between the two Adams, go through Romans 5:12-21 with two colored pencils, using one color to mark the sections that refer to the first Adam and the second color to mark those that speak of the Second Adam.

Romans 5:12 explains the consequences of Adam's disobedience recorded in Genesis 3: ". . . through one man sin entered into the world, and death through sin, and so death spread to all men . . . ."

Do you remember Humpty Dumpty, the egg with tiny arms and legs perched on the wall? He was in good shape until his great fall destroyed him. His ruin was complete — in spite of all the king's horses and all the king's men. If it had been a vase or bowl or figurine — or something else without life — that had shattered, it could have been glued together again. But not so with Humpty Dumpty. He contained something that no man could restore. In that "egg" was a germ of living substance that could have developed into a chicken. Man might be able to reconstruct the egg after a fashion, but bring back the life? No! Only God could create an egg with life in it — a living Humpty Dumpty.

This is a parable of man's experience. Adam once sat on the wall and had dominion over God's creation (Gen. 1:26). But Humpty Dumpty Adam fell from his high position and **died.** His spiritual death was complete. Ever since that time man has tried to fix up the mess by means of religion, culture, education, etc., but to no avail. It takes a **new birth** by faith in the Gospel of Jesus Christ. Adam tried to put Humpty Dumpty together with fig leaves, but to no avail. God alone has the answer to man's spiritual dilemma. Only He can restore life to the sinner.

"You Were There"

When Adam sinned, he was not the only one who died spiritually. The whole human race was involved. As the old CBS news drama declared, "You Were There." The Bible takes a collective view of the human race. The solidarity of humanity was represented by Adam as the federal head of the race. Indeed, the name Adam is the generic Hebrew word for humankind. Since all of us were represented by Adam, when he fell, we fell too. And the consequences of his fall are now the lot of the entire race: "death spread to all men, because all sinned . . ." (v. 12).

This passage is the foundation of what theologians call the doctrine of original sin. As a consequence of his disobedience, Adam's nature became sinful. Since he represented the human race, each of us is born with a sin nature. This doctrine is not well received by some people. Sinful people do not like to be told that they are sinners. They ask why they should bear the consequences of a choice made thousands of years ago by Adam in the Garden of Eden. But the Bible teaches that Adam's one act of disobedience changed the whole constitution of mankind and that mankind's marred nature, the sin nature, has been transmitted to every human being born since the time of Adam.

People in our highly individualistic society say, "It's not fair that I should suffer because of the bad choice of another." Yet we are all influenced by the choices of others. Read the story of Achan in Joshua 7 as an illustration of how the choice of one person affected many other people. No person is an island.

Furthermore, Paul anticipated this response, so he declares that "all sinned." Every time we sin, we demonstrate that if we had been in Adam's place in Eden, we also would have chosen to disobey.

Of course, many in our modern world find this unacceptable. Dr. Richard Halverson tells of a time when he used one of his own children as an illustration of original sin. Dr. Halverson reports:

> At the close of the service a young father who was getting his doctorate in psychology at the University of California in Los Angeles approached me. He was irked to say the least, that I had had the temerity to illustrate it with one of my children. When he finished his criticism, I asked him what he believed. He said he believed babies are born into the world morally neutral. "Can you demonstrate this?" I asked.
>
> "No," he answered.
>
> "You reject the doctrine of original sin because it cannot be demonstrated, but you accept this psychological view although it lacks any proof; how do you explain that?" I asked.
>
> Was not his hostility an example of human aversion to Biblical truth, rising from a built-in antipathy to God which is the essence of what is called original sin? I reminded him that not too many years ago we were being told by psychologists that babies were born into the world positively good and that only an unfortunate environment produced bad children. He said, "We don't believe that any more!" Psychology seems to get nearer and nearer to the Biblical doctrine of original sin.[2]

The acts of atrocity committed throughout human history verify the teaching that we are not born into the world morally neutral. As the Psalmist said, "Behold, I was brought forth in iniquity, and in sin my mother conceived me" (Ps. 51:5). Because of original sin, any attempts at human reformation by human means, no matter how creative or ingenious, are doomed to failure. We have inherited a sinful nature, and it is not within our power to refuse the inheritance. Sin and its consequences — spiritual and physical death — are universal.

Evidently some tried to refute Paul by teaching that there was no sin until the giving of the Law of Moses (vv. 13, 14). If there was no sin from Adam until Moses, that would nullify the teaching of original sin. But the law did not create sin. Rather it defined sin. It simply revealed more completely the principle of sin which was already in the world (cf. v. 20). The presence of death from Adam to Moses proves the presence of sin in everyone even before the law was given. The fact that everyone dies is the final proof of the truth of original sin. As a result of Adam's transgression, death, judgment, and condemnation were communicated to every human being.

Jesus Christ Reverses Adam's Legacy

All is lost if there is no man who can represent the whole human race and reverse the legacy of Adam. Jesus Christ is this Man — this Second Adam — and He stands in direct contrast to the first Adam. Paul begins to show this contrast in verse 14 and develops it throughout the remaining verses of the chapter. In these verses Paul goes back and forth between the two Adams to demonstrate how completely Jesus Christ counteracted the destructive consequences of Adam's sin.

Adam is called a figure (*KJV*), a type (*NASB*), a pattern (*NIV*) of Him who was to come (5:14). A "type" is an event or person in history that in certain characteristics and features corresponds with another event or person. Types may teach by presenting either similarities or contrasts. This type involves both. The similarity "consists in this, that Adam communicated to those whom he represented what belonged to him and that Christ also communicated to those whom he represented what belonged to him."[3] The contrast comes in the things communicated: Adam communicated sin, death, and condemnation; Jesus communicated righteousness, life, and justification as a gift of God's grace (5:15-21).

Jesus Christ raises us above our transgressions. He cancels

out the consequences of sin by giving us as a free gift a new nature to counteract the sin nature received from Adam. We become members of a new spiritual humanity of which Jesus Christ is the head. The Second Adam is able to do this because He was obedient. This provides another contrast with Adam, who was disobedient.

Adam was placed in the Garden of Eden, and God said, "It is perfect." Adam is the only human being who ever lived in a perfect environment. Until the serpent came, there was no negative influence in that environment. Only one condition was required of Adam and Eve. "Do not eat of the tree of knowledge of good and evil." Into this perfect environment where Adam and Eve enjoyed the presence of God and all His provision came the serpent bringing deception. He tempted them to distrust the word of God. "When you eat of that tree, you surely shall not die," he said. They listened to the seducer and disobeyed God. With that act of disobedience the curse came upon both mankind and the natural world.

Many, many years later God sent another Man, another representative of the human race into the world. In contrast to Adam's perfect environment of a plush garden, He came into a world filled with sin and all the atrocities of sin that had accumulated down through history. He came into a world in which there were false religions that had developed down through the years of man's spiritual darkness. He came into an environment where there was not only the deception of Satan, but also the deceit and animosity of the people around Him. He went out into the barren inferno of the Judean wilderness where He lived without food and drink for 40 days and 40 nights.

Jesus Triumphed Where Adam Failed

Jesus Christ did not come into a perfect environment. Yet, in the midst of an imperfect environment, He lived the perfect life. When Satan came to tempt Him, He resisted this deceiver and was obedient to God, obedient even unto death on the cross. That's the new Adam. That's Jesus Christ. And Paul said that as a result, those who place their faith and trust in Him, those who receive His grace, are made righteous in Him and brought into a new race of which He is the head.

God in His grace provided another Adam, a Second Adam, who succeeded where the first Adam had failed. ". . . but where sin increased, grace abounded all the more" (v. 20). The depravity, guilt, and alienation caused by Adam's sin which had accumulated in the human race were no match for the inexhaustible grace of God. Notice the "much mores" in (verses 15, 17, and 20). The tyrannical reign of death was overthrown by the benevolent reign of grace through righteousness (v. 21).

Dr. F.W. Borham tells the story of an old sailor named Sam Duncannon who retired from the Navy and took a job at a mission in one of our large cities. Duncannon himself had been won to Christ through the ministry of that mission. As a part of his personal ministry there, he bought beautiful pictures and took them into the dingy, dirty homes around the mission. This was his way of bringing a little bit of light into those homes.

"More to Follow"

Duncannon made it a practice to put a little saying under every picture before he gave it. At one of the mission services they sang this hymn, "Have you the Lord believed? Still there's more to follow. Of His grace have you received? Still there's more to follow." The three words "More to follow" stuck in Duncannon's mind. "I have to find a picture that will portray these words," he thought. A few days later he found a beautiful photograph of the water cascading over Niagara Falls. "That's the picture," he said. Not only is there an abundance of water coming over the falls, but there's more to follow."

What a beautiful picture of what God has done for us in Jesus Christ! His grace far surpasses the bondage and the penalities of sin. He gives us release, redemption, and deliverance. And there's more to follow, for the Book of Romans isn't over yet. How we live this life in Jesus Christ and the glory we experience in the Christian faith are still to be presented.

> His love has no limit, His grace has no measure,
> His power has no boundary known unto men;
> For out of His infinite riches in Jesus,
> He giveth and giveth and giveth again.

The end result of Christ's obedience is eternal life. Because of Adam, "the many" died, but the gift by the grace of the one Man, Jesus Christ, abounds to "the many" (v. 15; cf. vv. 18-19).

At this point Everett Harrison asks a pertinent question:

> Does the sweeping language used ("the many" being all
> men) suggest that all mankind will be brought within
> the circle of justification, so that none whatever will be
> lost? Some have thought so. But if the doctrine of univer-
> salism were being taught here, Paul would be contradict-
> ing himself, for he has already pictured men as perishing
> because of sin (2:12; cf. I Cor. 1:18). Furthermore, his en-
> tire presentation of salvation has emphasized the fact
> that justification is granted only on the basis of faith. We
> must conclude, therefore, that only as "the many" are
> found in Christ can they qualify as belonging to the
> righteous.[4]

By birth every human is in the first Adam and bears the
consequences of Adam's disobedience. But entrance into the
new humanity headed by the Second Adam, Jesus Christ, is
by faith.

A preacher was traveling on a train one day. He took the
window seat and began to read his Bible. As other passengers
boarded, they took all the seats except the one next to the
preacher. Nobody wanted to sit by a guy who was reading the
Bible. The last passenger came in and walked right past the
vacant seat. Suddenly he realized there weren't any other
seats. He would have to sit by the person reading the Bible.
So he sat as close to the aisle as he possibly could. The
preacher continued to read his Bible.

All of a sudden, the man burst out, "I suppose you're a
preacher!"

"Yes, I'm a preacher," came the reply.

Well, that was the worst thing the man could imagine. Here
he was seated by a preacher in a captive situation on a train.
What a horrible day this was going to be. Defensively he said,
"I suppose you believe God is going to send everybody to hell!"

"No, I don't believe God will send anybody to hell," the
preacher replied. The man was greatly relieved. At least this
preacher had some degree of intelligence.

But the preacher went on to explain, "No, sir, God will
never send anybody to hell. He has done everything He could
to keep men out. Over the very gate of hell is a cross, and on
that cross is a person. That person is Jesus Christ, the Son of
God, and you cannot get into hell without turning aside from
that person who hangs on the cross. He is there to keep you
out."

No wonder Paul said, ". . . as sin reigned in death, even so grace might reign through righteousness to eternal life **through Jesus Christ our Lord**" (v. 21, emphasis added). Verse 1 and verse 21 of Romans 5 both end with the phrase "through Jesus Christ our Lord." Through one man (the first Adam) sin and death entered the world (v. 12). Through another Man (the Second Adam) righteousness to eternal life becomes available to everyone who accepts Him by faith (v. 21). God formed us. Sin deformed us. Only Christ can transform us!

QUESTIONS FOR DISCUSSION

1. What examples of the concept of human solidarity can you give, in which one person acts and a group of people share the consequences?
2. In addition to the teaching of the Bible on the subject, what other evidence do we have that the sin of Adam affected every human being?
3. How might you answer a person who said, "It isn't fair that I should bear the consequences of the sin of Adam"?
4. How was the Second Adam like the first Adam? How was He different?
5. How was it possible for Jesus Christ to succeed where Adam failed?

THE LIFE
OF HOLY FAITH

CHAPTER NINE

DOES GRACE ALLOW US TO KEEP ON SINNING?

Romans 6:1-14

THE next major segment of Romans (chapters 6–8) deals primarily with what theologians call the doctrine of sanctification, that is, how we live our lives for Jesus Christ day by day and grow in His grace. The basis of our sanctification is the standing we have with God through Jesus Christ as a result of justification by faith (the topic of the section of Romans we have just completed).

The Question Raised

Chapter six begins with a question. To understand the source of this question, we must look again at Romans 5:20-21. In these two verses Paul concluded the section about the first and Second Adam with a great statement about the grace of God. He said that even though sin abounds and is always increasing, the grace of God superabounds. Regardless of the magnitude of the sin and transgression of mankind, the grace of God exceeds it.

This raised a question that Paul had dealt with many times in his preaching, and he answers this question in chapter six. The question is, "Does the grace of God allow us to keep on sinning?" (cf. 6:1).

The tremendous creativity and resourcefulness of mankind (some might call it the perversity of mankind's fallen nature) are revealed in many ways. Human perversity can take something very precious and make a travesty of it. Some people do

83

exactly that with the beautiful truth of the grace of God. God showed His abounding love to us by coming to us when we did not deserve it. He saved us even though there was nothing in us that warranted or merited our being saved. In His love and grace, He reached out to us. That's the victory of grace, and Paul described this victory by saying that where there was sin, grace superabounded. Grace was more than sufficient. The grace of God more than handled the tragic results of sin.

But some people who heard the Apostle Paul preach the grace of God began to reason this way: "Since Paul says that when there is more sin, then there is more grace, what we should do is sin all the more. For when we sin more, that will bring glory to God because it will allow more of God's grace to be manifested." Thus they used the very preciousness of the grace of God as an excuse to continue indulging their fallen natures and sinful desires. In this way they made a travesty of the magnificence of the grace of God. In Romans 6 Paul responds to these people.

Incidentally, such people were not found only in the first century; they are found in the 20th century as well. We still hear this argument being used with regard to certain sins. It is now used by some in the context of the contemporary problem of homosexuality. Some say that the homosexual, because of his practice, is a recipient of more of God's grace. Therefore, as he continues to indulge his homosexuality, he is actually exalting the grace of God. That's using the grace of God to justify continuing to sin. Is that the meaning of grace? Is it true that the more we sin, the more grace we will receive?

The Answer Given

How does the Apostle Paul respond to this perversion of the abounding grace of God? He asks, "What shall we say then? Are we to continue in sin that grace might increase?" (6:1). Paul gives the answer to this question in verse 2 in very forceful language. "May it never be!" The *King James Version* puts it this way, "Shall we continue in sin, that grace may abound? God forbid." Phillips paraphrases it: "Shall we sin to our heart's content and see how far we can exploit the grace of God? What a ghastly thought!" The *New English Bible* simply asks, "Should we sin all the more that grace might increase?" and answers, "No, No. We cannot respond to the grace of God in that way."

Because of Paul's directness, only the spiritually blind could miss or twist his answer. Paul follows this precise answer with a succinct explanation that reveals the irrationality of using the grace of God as license to indulge our sinful desires. The essense of his answer is in one sentence at the end of verse 2: "How shall we who died to sin still live in it?" The *NIV* puts it this way, "By no means! We died to sin; how can we live in it any longer?" Paul declares that Christians are dead to sin. If we are dead to sin, it makes no sense at all to say we're going to continue to live in sin.

The Answer Explained

Having given this succinct answer in verse 2, Paul goes on in the next paragraph to develop the rationale for his answer. In this paragraph he uses several means to explain the unity the Christian has with Christ, specifically in His death and resurrection. This unity is basic to Paul's response.

The first means Paul uses to demonstrate the believer's unity with Christ is the symbol of baptism (vv. 3, 4). What does baptism symbolize? It symbolizes death and burial. Baptism is a funeral of sorts — a symbolic funeral of the actual death of the old sin nature: ". . . we have been buried with Him through baptism into death . . ." (v. 4).

Every immersion baptism pictures a burial. The person goes into the water and is immersed. As he is immersed in the water, he is **buried** for that brief instant in the water. What does that picture? It symbolizes the death and burial of the old sin nature that was put to death with Christ on the cross. The old sin nature has died and is symbolically buried. For this reason some writers of past generations referred to the baptismal waters as the watery grave. Why did they use that kind of language? Because baptism portrays the death and burial of the old sin nature.

But more than death is pictured in baptism. There is also a picture of life. Not only did we die with Christ, but we were also raised with Christ. Notice the last part of verse 4: ". . . so we too might walk in newness of life." Not only is burial pictured in baptism; resurrection is also pictured. As the person who has been buried in the water comes out of the baptistry, he is dramatizing his spiritual resurrection. The old sin nature is left behind, buried, dead, gone. Now comes a change of direction in that person's life — a rising up to walk in the newness of life that is his in Jesus Christ. This means a new style of life, a new manner of life, a new set of priorities and values, a new conduct including new thoughts, new perspectives, and new behavior in a newness of life based on the power of Christ's resurrection. Thus Paul gives a symbolic explanation of his essential answer: the Christian is dead to sin. Since he is died to sin, it is morally incongruous that he would want to continue living in sin.

United With Christ

Having used the symbol of baptism to explain our unity with Christ, Paul goes on to talk about this relationship in actual terms. He says in verse 5: "For if we have become united with *Him* [Christ] in the likeness of His death, certainly we shall be also *in the likeness* of His resurrection . . . ." For the word translated "united," Paul uses a horticultural term. It is a word that was used for the engrafting of a branch into a tree. When you graft a nectarine branch into an orange tree, you cut a slit in the tree, place the end of the branch into the slit, and bind up the graft. After a time that tree will heal around the engrafted branch and the branch will become an integral part of the tree. The same life that flows through the tree will now flow through the branch. The branch will have become united with the tree.

The Apostle Paul says that as Christians we have been united with Christ — we have been grafted into Him. The life that is in Christ is now the life that flows through us. He says that we have been united with Christ in two major events: His death and His resurrection. Because of our union with Christ, we can actually say that we were present both at Christ's crucifixion and at the open tomb on Easter Sunday morning. In some way, by God's power, we were by faith united with Christ at those momentous events.

I noted in the last chapter that when some people read in Romans 5 that in Adam all sinned and all died, they object, saying that it is not fair that we should bear the consequences of Adam's sin. But Romans 6 continues to show how this is balanced by the new Adam, Jesus Christ. Just as we were united with the first Adam in the Garden of Eden, even so we were in union with the Second Adam in the Garden of Resurrection. When Christ died, we died. We died to sin. When Christ rose, we rose. We rose to live a new life in Him.

Paul says this is actual. We are united with Christ in His death and in His resurrection. Therefore, how could we possibly want to continue in sin. It is totally incongruous that a person who is united with Christ and shares His life would abuse the grace of God by using that grace as an excuse to sin.

Paul continues his detailed explanation of these truths in verses 6-11 by making them personal. Notice his use of personal pronouns in this section. Take your pencil and mark all his uses of we, our, your, yourselves, etc. Paul personalizes the fact that our old self has been put to death. Therefore, we need no longer serve it.

In verses 6 and 7 he personalizes this truth in three ways. First, he says *our* old self was crucified. This same truth is taught in Colossians 3:9. This is another way of stating that the old sin nature has died. Nevertheless, the old man seeks to dominate the believer, as Ephesians 4:22 implies and experience confirms. Everett Harrison speculates, "It is possible that what has been crucified with Christ is our place in Adam, our position in the old creation, which is under the sway of sin and death. For the Christian, the old is gone; he belongs to the new creation order (II Cor. 5:17)."[1]

Second, Paul says that our body of sin has been done away with (v. 6). The body is a vehicle of sin in the sense that many of the temptations to sin come to us through the physical body. But now Paul says that this is done away with. The word he uses here means that the body no longer has any control. It means that the body is rendered inactive with regard to sin. The temptation that comes to us through the power of the body is now neutralized. It's like a clutch and gearbox. When we push in the clutch, the gears are disengaged. As a result, even though the engine is running, its power has no effect on the vehicle. It will not respond.

This is a picture of one of the results of our union with Christ. Christ has pushed in the clutch on the power of the sin that comes to us through the body. The old nature may speak. It may tempt us. But we need not respond. We are no longer slaves of sin.

Paul's third explanation of this truth is given in verse 7: We have been freed from sin because of our death in Christ. The wages of sin is death. When sin is committed, the wage must be paid; and that wage is death. But when Jesus Christ died on the cross for us, we also died on that cross in Him. Therefore, the death penalty for our sin has now been paid. Since the penalty has been paid, freedom comes as a result. We have been set free from the power of sin. Why would we want to sin since we have been set free?

Having explained the results of our union with Christ *in His death*, Paul turns in verses 8-10 to the correlative truth. He explains what it means *to be risen* with Christ. Our resurrection with Christ means two things. First, it means that death is conquered forever. The power of sin has been forever vanquished. The power of spiritual death will never be manifested upon a Christian again.

Second, having been raised with Christ means that the life of God is in us, and we now live to God.

Consequences of These Truths

What are the consequences of these truths in our daily lives? Paul answers that question in verses 11-14. Because we have died in Christ and have risen in Him, we should *consider* ourselves dead to sin but alive to God in Jesus Christ.

By using the word "consider" in this verse, Paul emphasizes the importance of the mind as a motivator of our behavior. Earlier in this chapter he used the word "know" several times (vv. 3, 6, 9). We *know* that we have died to Christ; we *know* that we've been made alive to Christ. Now he says, "consider," that is, think about it, meditate upon it, calculate it. Consider what it means to be dead in Christ and alive in Him.

Bruce Larson tells of a young man who was participating in a small group meeting. The leader asked group members to share the most exciting thing that had happened to them in the last two weeks. This young man jumped right out of his chair and said, "The most exciting thing that's happened to me in the last two weeks is that I had my handwriting analyzed. When my handwriting analysis came back, it said that I was an extrovert. Here I've been an introvert all my life. I've been afraid to speak. I've been afraid of crowds. But my handwriting said I'm an extrovert. And since that day, I've been acting like an extrovert. Now I'm an extrovert."

Here is an illustration of the awesome power of the mind. Because of the handwriting analysis, this man began to consider himself an extrovert, and his behavior changed. Paul says, "Consider what this means that we are dead in Christ and alive in Him."

John R. Stott says that the autobiography of every Christian has two volumes:

> The first volume would be all of your life in your unregenerated self. It would be all of your pre-Christian life. How does that first volume end? Volume one ends with a death. It ends with the death of that unregenerate nature, of that old sin nature. Now it is time for volume two. How does volume two begin? Volume two begins with a resurrection — the resurrection of Jesus Christ. But it is also your resurrection because you were united with Christ. It's the gift of new life to you in the new birth experience. Volume one is full of sin and death. Volume two is the resurrection and life towards God.[2]

Paul says, "Consider . . . ," that is, think about what this means. And then he says, if you have been dead and now are alive to God through Jesus Christ — now just stop and think about this, with volume two going and you experiencing all the excitement of growing in the resurrection life in Christ — do you ever want to go back to volume one? Who would want to go back to volume one?

So does grace mean that we can keep on sinning, that we can live back in volume one? Most certainly not. Instead grace closed volume one with the death of Jesus Christ. Furthermore, grace opened up volume two with the resurrection of Jesus Christ, and through the grace of God we are allowed to participate in His resurrection life. Consider this, Paul says.

Therefore Christians must not allow sin to reign in them. Instead we must yield, surrender, and present the very members of our bodies to God. Don't present them as instruments of unrighteousness, but instead present them as instruments of righteousness to God (v. 13). What God has made alive, present to Him.

The word "present" ("yield," *KJV*) indicates a critical resolve, a decision of surrender. Because of our union with Christ, when we are tempted to sin, we do not need to obey the old master. We have been given a new power — the power of the resurrection life of Jesus Christ. Therefore when temptation comes, we can voluntarily, deliberately, and willfully say to its voice, "I am not your servant any longer. I do not need to listen to you!" When temptation comes, go back to Romans 6 and say, "I'm dead to that. It doesn't have any power or control or authority over me anymore." When you "consider" this, it will change your perspective about the power of the temptation. You are dead to sin. Consider it, think about it. Present yourself alive to God.

The story is told of a town misfit who died. After his funeral they began the procession to the cemetery. On the way they passed the tavern where this man had imbibed to drunkenness night after night. But on this particular trip by the tavern, he didn't go in. His body no longer had any desire for alcohol. Continuing on, the procession went by the racetrack where he had squandered many of his paychecks betting on the horses in the hope that he would pick a winner and find the pot of gold at the end of the racetrack. But this time as he went by, he had no desire to stop and gamble. Next the procession went by the X-rated theater where he had seen many pornographic movies. But this time he did not respond to the seductive marquee. It incited no desires in his body at all. Finally, the procession passed his neighbor's house. He and his neighbor had fought, squabbled, and bickered for years. More than once he had given his neighbor a piece of his mind and lashed him with his tongue. But this time as he went by there was no anger or hostility toward his neighbor generated in his heart. Why? **Because he was dead.**

Spiritually speaking, Christians are also dead, because we died in Christ. Therefore, we do not need to respond to the desires that are rooted in the sin nature. We are dead to them in Jesus Christ. Since this is true, does it make any sense that we should want to pervert the grace of God as an excuse to keep on sinning? By no means! May it never be! God forbid! What a ghastly idea! Instead, we must surrender ourselves to God. He has given you power in your body to serve Him. Therefore, yield every aspect of your personality and life potential as well as the individual parts of your body to the service of God and to righteousness. Grace is not an excuse to sin. Quite the contrary, grace has annihilated sin's control and mastery over us (v. 14).

QUESTIONS FOR DISCUSSION

1. Is the idea that the grace of God allows us to keep on sinning still with us today? What examples can you give of those who either teach or imply that this is true?

2. Do we need more emphasis in our churches on the *meaning* of baptism? If so, why?

3. In what sense have we been united with Christ in His

death? In what sense have we been united with Him in His resurrection?

4. To what extent is our behavior motivated by our minds? By our emotions? What part *should* each play?
5. What tactics does this chapter give us for dealing with temptation?

CHAPTER TEN

WHEN SLAVERY IS GOOD

Romans 6:15—7:6

JUSTIFICATION AND SANCTIFICATION — you could listen for years to the conversations on the sidewalks of your town or city and probably never hear these two words used. They are not a part of the vocabulary of secular America. Yet these two words are crucial concepts in the gospel according to Paul. After demonstrating that all people are sinners, Paul presented God's answer to man's dilemma in terms of justification (3:21—5:20). Through Jesus Christ we have been set free from the penalty of sin, as Romans 5 demonstrates.

But Jesus Christ does more. He also sets believers free from the power of indwelling sin. That's sanctification, and it is the theme of Romans 6, 7, and 8. Justification happens because grace reaches into our lives in Christ. Sanctification happens when grace reigns on a daily basis in our lives. Grace is more than pardon from sin. It is power over sin. F.F. Bruce points out the relationship between justification and sanctification: "Those who have been justified are now being sanctified: if a man is not being sanctified, there is no reason to believe that he has been justified."[1]

The Relationship Between Justification and Sanctification

Everett F. Harrison explains the relationship between justification and sanctification with this helpful diagram, to which I have added a few explanatory terms:[2]

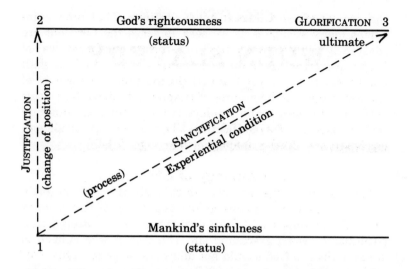

When a person believes on the Lord Jesus Christ, he both makes an immediate positional change and begins a process. The dashed line between numbers 1 and 2 represents the change in position. This change takes place when God declares the new believer to be righteous on the basis of the fact that the righteousness of Christ has been imputed to him. This change of status is justification. This does not mean that the person is experientially sinless or mature, for he is just a newborn baby spiritually speaking.

But at the point of conversion the person also begins a process of spiritual growth which the Bible calls sancification. This process takes place as the believer walks in the Spirit and develops the fruit of the Spirit in his daily life.

The process includes understanding and expressing in daily conduct the new nature the believer now has because of his union with Christ. Point 3 on the diagram represents the goal of the process of sanctification, when the believer is fully conformed not only positionally but experientially to the image of Christ (Rom. 8:29). At that point he will have not only a righteous status because of the righteousness of Christ, but also a completely righteous character as the redemptive work of Christ is completed in every aspect of his being.

The *culmination* of the process of sanctification will occur only at death (Heb. 12:23) or at the return of Christ for those saints still alive at His coming (I Jn. 3:2). In the meantime, the *process* of sanctification must continue. That process includes many struggles as we seek to serve the Lord but are constantly tempted by the flesh to return to our former way of living. Nevertheless, Paul declares that even now "sin shall not be master over you" (6:14). He continues in the rest of chapter 6 and the beginning of chapter 7 to drive home this point. In this section he employs two analogies to illustrate certain aspects of sanctification: (1) the analogy of slavery (6:15-23), and (2) the analogy of marriage (7:1-6).

The Analogy of Slavery

The questions and response which begin this section (6:15-23) are similar to the ones at the beginning of this chapter (vv. 1-2). In verses 1-14 Paul demonstrated the utter incompatibility between grace and sin. The person who is dead to sin and alive to God should not allow sin to reign in his mortal body. Now in verses 15-23 Paul continues to show the incompatibility between grace and sinning, using the picture of slavery.

The term "servants" used in the King James Version can be misleading. Paul is not talking about a hired servant who is free to come and go when he is not working for his employer. He is talking about a slave who is completely subject to the will of his master. The one the slave obeys is his master, and an outside observer could soon tell which slaves belonged to which masters simply by observing the master each slave obeyed.

In a similar way, we are slaves to the spiritual master we obey. When we sin, we are obeying Satan. As Jesus said, ". . . every one who commits sin is the slave of sin" (Jn. 8:34). Until grace through Jesus Christ entered the picture, we had no choice but to do all the evil things that sin wanted us to do. But now Christ has set us free from the bondage of sin and its law of death. As Christians we now have the ability to choose which master we will obey. We do this by "presenting" ourselves as "slaves for obedience" (v. 16). Slavery is inevitable, for we will either be slaves to sin or slaves to righteousness, and our conduct reveals the identity of our master.

In the remaining verses of Romans 6 Paul contrasts the two kinds of slavery. The grid at the top of the next page diagrams the contrast.

In verses 17 and 18 Paul contrasts the two kinds of slavery

The Master 6:17, 18, 22	Sin	God righteousness
The Process 6:19, 21, 22	impurity, lawlessness, shame	sanctification
The Outcome 6:21-23	death	life

as to their beginnings. "Though you were slaves of sin" indicates that our slavery to sin began at birth. This slavery comes from the sin nature we inherit as children of the first Adam. But slavery to God begins with an obedient response from the heart to the message of the gospel of grace ("that form of teaching to which you were committed," v. 17). At the moment this response is made, the obedient believer is set free from his old master, Sin (throughout this section sin is personified as a horrible monster who is master over his slaves), and becomes a slave of a new master, God. Since a slave's former owner has no authority over him when he becomes someone else's property, the new believer no longer needs to respond to his old master, Sin. He now needs to obey only his new master, God.

Paul's next step is to contrast the two kinds of slavery with regard to their development (v. 19). As Jesus said, No person can serve two masters. Therefore the person who used to "present" his members to the master, Sin, must now "present" his members with at least equal devotion and diligence to the service of his new master, God. Acts of obedience to each master set in motion a process. Serving sin results in a grim process of moral deterioration. Acts of impurity and lawlessness generate further like acts. This process leads to total destruction — moral, spiritual, emotional, intellectual, physical.

Obedience to God, on the other hand, sets in motion a gloriously different process — one of moral sanctification, purity, and righteous conduct. Each kind of slavery develops. Neither is static. In one, the person becomes increasingly worse. In the other, the person gets better and better. With each act of sin the soul is preconditioned to yield more easily to the next. With each sinful act, Sin's tyrannical control is tightened.

But salvation reverses this process in our lives. With each act of yielding to the known will of God, we are preconditioned to more easily yield to His will the next time. Each act of yielding to God serves to strengthen His control in our lives. Thus with increasing acceleration we are progressively transformed into His image of righteousness. This is practical holiness through the process of progressive sanctification. God's grace has given us the freedom to choose this process of sanctification instead of being hopelessly enslaved to the process which leads to shame.

Finally, the two kinds of slavery are radically opposite in their ultimate outcome. Slavery to Sin results in death, both physical and spiritual death. But slavery to God and righteousness results in life eternal. Sin presents a horrible paycheck to its slaves — death. But God presents as a free gift eternal life to those who are in Jesus Christ. Eternal life is a *charisma* (gift of grace) from God. This is the word from which our word "charismatic" is derived. The true charismatic is the person who by faith has received God's gift of eternal life. And the "sign" gift of the genuine charismatic is obedience, which clearly shows that the person is a slave of God.

Freedom Through Slavery

The outcome of slavery to God is not only eternal life, but also genuine freedom. The paradox of the gospel is that we cannot be truly free until we are enslaved to God through Jesus Christ. This is God's gracious doing. Jesus said, ". . . you shall know the truth, and the truth shall make you free. . . . If therefore the Son shall make you free, you shall be free indeed" (Jn. 8:32, 36). Slavery to sin is bondage. Slavery to God is freedom, and that makes slavery to Him good.

Recently a woman complained to me that as a child and during her teenage years she was dominated by her mother. "Now," she said, "I'm married and I'm dominated by my husband. All I did was exchange one slavery for another." Her voice reeked with resentment, indicating that she was less than thrilled with either "master."

For us slavery is inevitable, but by God's grace we have been given the opportunity to switch masters. If we Christians ever resent being enslaved to God, we expose either our ignorance or, worse yet, our lack of gratitude regarding the magnitude of God's grace, which made the switch in masters a reality. As slaves of God, would we want to continue to sin? Absolutely not! Rather, as slaves of God we are committed to obeying Him. As slaves of God we have freedom which equips us to serve the living God.

The Analogy of Marriage

Even though we now move into the next chapter (Romans 7), this paragraph (vv. 1-6) continues the major topic of Romans 6, i.e., the meaning of our union with Christ in His death and resurrection as it relates to both our character and our conduct as Christians. The analogy which Paul employs in this paragraph illustrates the powerful point of 6:14: "For sin shall not be master over you, for you are not under law, but under grace." The slavery analogy of the previous paragraph (6:15-23) showed that sin should not be our master because we are now slaves of a new master. The marriage analogy of this paragraph speaks to the last part of Romans 6:14 by showing why Christians are no longer under the law. Paul uses the analogy of marriage to illustrate specifically the principle that death cancels previous obligations. The words "released from the law" are used both in the analogy itself (v. 2) and in the application of the analogy (v. 6). In both instances it was a death that effected the release.

The analogy itself is presented in 7:1-3. The point Paul wanted to make would be easily understood by anyone who knew the workings of law, whether Jewish or Roman. Law has limited jurisdiction. Only the living can respond to its requirements. A dead person can neither obey nor disobey the law. For instance, even the laws regarding a covenant as essential and sacred as the marriage covenant specify that death releases either partner, in this case the wife, from the obligation of fidelity inherent in marriage.

If a married woman is joined to another man while her husband is still alive, she is an adulteress. But if the husband dies, she is both legally and ethically free to marry another man. The husband's death *releases* her from the jurisdiction of the marriage law, and she is no longer required to fulfill the obligation it placed upon her. The death of her husband totally alters the rules. Now she can marry another man and not become an adulteress. Because of her husband's death, she is now "free from the law" (v. 3).

The "therefore" in verse 4 tells us that Paul is now ready to make the application of this illustration. He declares, ". . . my brethren, you also were made to die to the Law . . ." (v. 4). Paul's point was that death results in release. Therefore, if Christians have died to the law, we must conclude that, as a result, "we have been released from the Law" (v. 6).

But we are still alive. Otherwise I couldn't have written these words and you couldn't be reading them! So when and where did the death that released us occur? Paul answers that question by stating that we died "through the body of Christ" (v. 4) when He died on the cross (remember 6:3-10). Christ's death not only freed us from sin, it also released us from the jurisdiction of the law.

Spiritually this means that we are not only released from our obligations to the law, we are also joined to the resurrected Christ in a marriage which is to bear fruit. Jesus taught the same blessed truth to His disciples: "he who abides in Me, and I in him, he bears much fruit . . ." (Jn. 15:5). Believers, as the bride of Christ, are spiritually married to a resurrected husband, Jesus Christ. Abundant progeny must result from this union, as many others experience the life-giving power of Christ in their spirits. This fruit is radically different from that which we previously produced (v. 5). Then the law aroused the passions of our flesh (our sinful nature), which went to work in our bodies and produced a horrendous fruit, namely death.

Release from the law means that its demands have been satisfied through the death of Christ. Release from the law means that it is now powerless to accuse us and condemn us. But release from the law does not mean that we are no longer obligated to obey God's moral law. Union with the Spirit, however, brings an entirely new motivation and power for righteous living, which the law could never provide.

Christians operate according to an entirely new principle. Instead of striving to measure up to an external standard of righteousness, we yield ourselves to the indwelling Holy Spirit, who expresses Himself from within. The moral law is now internalized, written on the hearts of believers by the Spirit (Jer. 31:33, 34; Heb. 10:15-18). Now the Spirit supplies from within the heart the regulative principle that the law formerly and imperfectly supplied from without.

If someone placed before me paintings created by Rembrandt, da Vinci, or Michelangelo and commanded me to paint identical pictures, I would be totally unable to do so. You could even give me art lessons, but it would still be an impossible command for me, because I have no talent for painting. But if the genius of these men could be placed within me, I would then be able to paint masterpieces too. Without this, the paintings by these masters only reveal my total lack of artistic ability and heighten my frustration over my inability to perform. They cannot make me an artist. Only the receiving of a new genius could do that.

In a similar way, the "oldness of the letter" (the law, v. 6) cannot create righteous behavior, because the real problem is the condition of the human heart. The new Spirit we receive as Christians through the new birth solves that problem. (Romans 8:1-27 will present greater detail on the "newness of the Spirit," who now motivates our service.) The death of Christ is the basis for our release from the law. The resurrection of Christ is the basis for the newness of the Spirit, who now empowers our lives for obedience and holiness.

With these two analogies, one from slavery and the other from marriage, Paul continues to teach us that even though we are no longer under the law, sin must not have mastery over us. Instead we are under grace — a grace that unites us with Christ in His death and resurrection. As a result we are dead to the old master, Sin, and have come alive to a new master, God. Therefore, in obedience to the new master, we will not sin. Likewise, because of our union with Christ through faith, we are no longer married to the letter of the law, which brings death. Instead we are married to the risen Christ, who indwells us by His Spirit. Therefore, the Christian life is serving the risen Christ in the power of the Holy Spirit, "bearing fruit in every good work" (Col. 1:10).

QUESTIONS FOR DISCUSSION

1. How are justification and sanctification related? How are they different?
2. Why is slavery inevitable? What determines which master we serve?
3. What kind of fruit results from our marriage to the resurrected Jesus Christ?
4. What does it mean to us to be released from the law? What does it not mean?
5. When *is* slavery good? Why is it good?

CHAPTER ELEVEN

WHY WE HAVE TROUBLE KEEPING OUR NEW YEAR'S RESOLUTIONS

Romans 7:7-25

T HE ritual takes place annually. Every New Year's Eve or New Year's Day, someone encourages us to evaluate our lives and then make resolutions to improve ourselves in the coming year. We make our resolutions in all sincerity, perhaps even writing them down so that we can review them in a month or two to see how we are doing.

What were your last New Year's resolutions? That's the simple question to answer. The harder question is, "Have you kept your resolutions?" How about that resolution to lose some weight? Are you still saying, "I'll start my diet tomorrow"? Or how about that resolve not to have such a short fuse? Are you controlling your temper, or have you exploded a few times since making that resolution? Any conscientious person has struggled with keeping resolutions. One person was so frustrated by his failure to fulfill his resolutions that last New Year's he resolved never to make any more New Year's resolutions. So far, he's kept that one.

From our experiences with resolutions, we know that though the resolve is the first step, it does not in itself guarantee a change in behavior. Frequently there is a big gap between what we intend and what we do. In the light of what Paul has said about our freedom from slavery to sin and our release from the law, why aren't we Christians more obedient to our Lord? Why don't we keep our resolutions? If we have victory over sin, why must we continually battle it?

In Romans 7:7-25, Paul gives us some answers to these questions. In this passage he deals with the struggle that characterizes the process of sanctification. So far he has explained what actually happens when a sinner is identified with Christ through faith. But because we still live in the body, we continue to experience the onslaughts of the sin nature. In one respect the conflict *intensifies* when we become Christians, for we now have two diametrically opposed natures within us. We often feel as if a civil war is taking place within us. And, indeed, such is the case, "For the flesh sets its desire against the Spirit, and the Spirit against the flesh; for these are in opposition to one another . . ." (Gal. 5:17).

When this battle intensifies, some Christians begin to question the reality of Christ's redemptive work in their lives. Others may feel that they are failures as Christians because they have these conflicts. They may think that a genuine Christian has no battles with the flesh, and that since they do, something is wrong with them. As a result, they may become discouraged, wave the white flag of surrender to the flesh, and backslide into sin.

In this intensely autobiographical section, the Apostle Paul describes his battle with the flesh as he continued down the road of sanctification to Christian maturity. Notice how many times he uses first person pronouns — I, me, my — in these verses. In this candid section the apostle wrote the spiritual biography of Everyperson. If a Christian as great as Paul experienced this inner conflict between the two natures, then you and I should not allow such a conflict within us to cause us to quit living as Christians. In these verses Paul relives a crucial period in his life. By exposing the struggles of *his* soul, he helps us understand *ours*.

Evidently Paul also had trouble, at least at times, keeping his New Year's resolutions. Why? Paul's first response to this question relates to the way indwelling sin responds to the law (vv. 7-13). His second response relates to carnality in the life of the Christian (vv. 14-25).

Sin and the Law

John R.W. Stott has identified three attitudes toward the law which are interwoven in Romans 7.

1. The legalist is a man in bondage to the law. He imagines that his relationship to God depends on his obedi-

ence to it. And as he seeks to be justified by the works of
the law, he finds the law a harsh and inflexible task-
master. . . .
2. The antinomian (sometimes synonymous with liber-
tine) goes to the other extreme. He rejects the law al-
together, and even blames it for most of man's moral and
spiritual problems.
3. The law-abiding believer preserves the balance. He
recognizes the weakness of the law (Romans 8:3 . . .) . . .
that it can neither justify nor sanctify us because in ourselves we are not capable of obeying it. Yet the law-abiding believer delights in the law as an expression of the
will of God, and seeks by the power of the indwelling
Spirit to obey it.[1]

In verses 7-14 Paul uses verbs in the past tense, while in
verses 14-25 he uses verbs in the present tense. In the first of
these two paragraphs he describes the problem he had in his
former life as a legalist, for Paul was a "Pharisee of the
Pharisees" (the ultimate legalist).

Problems of the Legalist

The legalist has some grave problems brought about by the
relationship between sin and the law. First, although the law
itself certainly is not sinful, it does define and reveal sin: "I
would not have come to know sin except through the law . . ."
(v. 7). Paul states that he did not know there was such a thing
as covetousness until the law said, "You shall not covet." Evidently Paul is using the tenth and final commandment as an
illustration of all the commandments.

Several streets in our town have been changed from two-
way to one-way traffic. This change in the law redefined what
was legal and illegal. One day you could legally travel either
way on these streets. But the next day, if you went the wrong
way, you were doing something illegal. In a similar way, the
rules of a game define violations, and penalties are attached
to each violation. And in a moral sense, the law defined sin.

But even more than this, Paul says that the law stimulates
sin into action by provoking illicit desire. This is the second
problem for the legalist. Actually it was sin (literally *the* sin
— Paul personifies sin here) that produced coveting of every
kind in Paul, but the commandment gave sin the "opportunity" (a military term meaning a beachhead, a place from
which to launch an attack) to become active. Because of the
commandment, sin became alive. Until the commandment

came along, sin had been lying down, like a sleeping lion. But the command which forbids coveting aroused the monster, sin, into action. Up until that time his sin nature had been relatively dormant. But since sin is basically disobedience, the law raised the consciousness of sin by bringing into expression the sin which was already in his heart.

Watchman Nee uses the example of a clumsy servant to illustrate this point. As long as the clumsy servant sits still and does nothing, his clumsiness is not apparent. But the minute you ask him to get up and do something, the trouble begins. He knocks over the chair as he stands up. He trips over the footstool when he starts to walk. He drops a precious dish when he tries to serve from it. He spills paint on the new carpet. But his clumsiness wasn't noticed until you made demands on him. He was clumsy even while sitting down, but it was not revealed until you asked him to do something.

Nee concludes, "We are all sinners by nature. If God asks nothing of us, all seems to go well, but as soon as He demands something of us, the occasion is provided for a grand display of our sinfulness . . . when a holy law is applied to sinful man. Then it is that his sinfulness comes out in full display."[2]

The Penalty on Sin Is Death

For this reason the legalist is doomed not only to frustration, but also to defeat, for the law pronounces a death penalty on sin (vv. 10, 11). This is the third problem for the legalist. When Paul was blissfully ignorant of the law's demands, perhaps during his early childhood, he was spiritually alive (v. 9). But with knowledge of the law came spiritual death. The law had promised life, saying, "Do this and you shall live" (see Lev. 18:5). But instead it brought spiritual death to Paul. Why? Because sin used the law as a base of operations from which to deceive Paul and from which ultimately to kill him by bringing spiritual death.

The same pattern occurred in the Garden of Eden. All was good in the Garden, but the command was given, ". . . from the tree of the knowledge of good and evil you shall not eat . . ." (Gen. 2:17). Satan used this very command, scorning its penalty of death, to deceive Eve and kill her spiritually (Gen. 3:1-13). The word "deceive" (Rom. 7:11) pictures sin luring its victim off of the main highway onto a dark side road and then mercilessly killing that victim. Sin deceives by promising power, pleasure, and wisdom (Gen. 3:5-6), but all it can really offer is death.

Evidently some people, upon hearing Paul's words, concluded that things would have been much better if the law had never been given. They accused the law itself of being sinful. Therefore, Paul asks, "Is the Law sin?" (v. 7); to which he gives the authoritative response, "May it never be!" Then he states with firm conviction that "the Law is holy, and the commandment is holy and righteous and good" (v. 12). The law is not the cause of spiritual death. Rather, sin is the villain. Indeed, sin is such a despicable monster that it takes advantage of something good, the law, and uses it as a means for doing its dastardly work. The law reveals how despicable and perverted sin is. Sin's goal is spiritual death, and it will use any means to achieve that goal.

We have trouble keeping our New Year's resolutions because sin uses them the same way it uses the law — to reveal, provoke, and condemn.

The Problem of Carnality

The problem of carnality is a second reason why Christians have trouble keeping their resolutions. As I mentioned earlier, Paul switches verb tenses in verse 14, changing from past tense to present tense, which he uses throughout the rest of the chapter. But he continues to use first person pronouns as he describes the inner conflict of the carnal Christian who seeks to live the Christian life using only his own human resources rather than the divine resources of the Holy Spirit. By using the first person, Paul may have been describing the times he attempted to live for Christ on his own. But he also may have been using a literary device that enables us to easily identify with what he is saying.

Since most Christians slip all too easily into carnality (cf. I Cor. 3:3ff.), we can readily identify with the warfare that Paul describes in these verses. The conflict centers around the fact that a Christian joyfully concurs with the law of God in his inner person, but experiences a different law at work in the members of his body, which wage war against the law of the renewed mind (vv. 22-23). Paul must be speaking here of *Christian* experience, for only Christians have the law of God written on their hearts and in their minds, which have been renewed as a result of the new birth. But the sinful nature still wages war, and hence the conflict.

Some time ago a homeowner in Jacksonville, Florida, discovered a unique skink (a kind of lizard). What made this skink unusual was that it had two heads, one at each end of its body. What a picture of absolute frustration this skink was! When it tried to run, its legs actually moved in opposite directions.

This is a striking caricature of the carnal Christian — the Christian who is trying to go his own way and still serve God. The Christian now has the mind of Christ, but he also still has the mind of the flesh, which is hostile toward God (Rom. 8:7). If the believer does not completely submit himself to Christ but tries to serve self as well, he becomes a spiritual schizophrenic. He resembles the two-headed skink trying to go in opposite directions at the same time.

In this passage Paul describes the experience of an anguished soul who is in a state of tension because he lives in two worlds. He lives simultaneously on two planes, eagerly longing to live on the higher plane of the new spiritual nature of the resurrected Christ, but sadly aware of the constant bombardments of indwelling sin that keep pulling him down to a lower plane. These two planes are identified in v. 14: "the Law is spiritual; but I am of flesh." Paul speaks as a Christian who has enough maturity to have a clear view both of his own sin nature and of God's holy law. Here, then, is another area of conflict, the conflict between that which is spiritual and that which is of the flesh—carnal (cf. Gal. 5:17; I Cor. 2:10-3:3).

In verses 14-20 Paul elaborates on this conflict by showing that his good intentions do not always result in actions which are obedient to God's holy law, even though he desires very much that they should. In verses 18-20 he basically repeats what he said in verses 14-17. Perhaps he does this for emphasis. But perhaps it also reveals the intensity with which he feels the inner conflict. People under pressure often repeat themselves.

In each section Paul frankly acknowledges his condition when he relies only on himself. He has no strength of his own to fight off the assaults of the sin nature (v. 14). The "we know" of verse 14 is matched by the "I know" of verse 18. And his statement, "For I know that nothing good dwells in me, that is, in my flesh . . ." (v. 18), expresses essentially the same idea as verse 14. Paul says that if he relies only on himself, even though he is a Christian, he remains in captivity to the carnal nature. The same is true for us. Paul is speaking for every Christian.

Each of these two sections also vividly describes the resulting conflict (cf. v. 15 with vv. 18 and 19). Paul finds himself doing things which he, as a Christian, actually detests. Instead of doing the good that he wishes to do, he does exactly the opposite. He does what he does not wish to do. He wills to do what is right, but in himself he cannot do it.

> Let me stress again that this is the conflict of a Christian man, who knows the will of God, loves it, wants it, yearns to do it, but who finds that still *by himself* he cannot do it. His whole being (his mind and his will) is set upon the will of God and the law of God. He longs to do good. He hates to do evil — hates it with a holy hatred. And if he does sin, it is against his mind, his will, his consent; it is against the whole tenor of his life. Herein lies the conflict of the Christian.[3]

Each of these two essentially parallel sections concludes with a statement about the cause of the Christian's inability in himself. The reason I can't do what I want to do is because of "sin which indwells me" (vv. 17, 20). If, when he became a Christian, Paul thought that he would never sin again, that naiveté has been shattered. He has discovered that "evil is present in me, the one who wishes to do good" (v. 21). His will has been reoriented toward God and His holy law, but many of his actions are still controlled by the flesh. In this situation of war between the "law of my mind" and the "law of sin" (v. 23), the problem is that the members of the physical body are allied with indwelling sin (v. 22-23). Therefore this battle will continue in varying degrees until our mortal, physical body is redeemed from the curse of sin. At present our spirits and our minds are redeemed; but the body still awaits its redemption (cf. Rom. 8:23). Until then sin will use our physical members as avenues through which to attack us. Therefore we experience this warfare taking place within our bodies and we long for relief. We cry out with Paul, "Wretched man that I am! Who will set me free from the body of this death?" (v. 24). Our spirits are free. Our minds are free. Oh, that our bodies were also set free from death, the wages of sin!

This cry of Paul (v. 24) may have a historical picture behind it. The Roman poet Virgil wrote that the Etruscan king

Mezentius tied decomposing human corpses on the backs of his living captives. As a result, the stench of decay was always with them. Soon the decomposing bodies also caused horrendous sores on the living person. These sores would become infected. Gangrene would set in, and the captive would die a slow, agonizing death. He would cry out to be set free from the decaying body on his back, but no one was allowed to release him.

Christ Provides the Answer

Spiritually speaking, we join Paul in crying out for deliverance from the body of death. Do we have someone who liberates us from this conflict? YES! "Thanks be to God through Jesus Christ our Lord!" (v. 25). Paul does not immediately expand on this statement, but it is like an index finger pointing to the next chapter, Romans 8, which will reveal God's answer so that the Christian doesn't have to live in constant conflict between his intentions and his actions. Unfortunately, many Christians have not discovered that answer and are trying to do the impossible — live the Christian life by their own strength and ingenuity.

The last part of verse 25 is a summary statement of the principle developed in verses 14-25. Paul wrote this entire section to expose the no-goodness and weakness of our flesh. Now he will move on to show us that only the Holy Spirit can deliver us from the flesh and empower us for victorious Christian living.

Praise God, the futility of Romans 7, though all to common in the experience of many Christians, is not what God intended. God's plan includes a power to indwell us that is stronger than the power of indwelling sin. Romans 8 will unfold for us the person, purpose, and power of the indwelling Holy Spirit. We have trouble keeping our New Year's resolutions when we live in the carnality described in Romans 7:14-25 rather than in the power of the Holy Spirit described in Romans 8.

QUESTIONS FOR DISCUSSION

1. In the light of this chapter, is it okay for Christians to make New Year's resolutions? What problems might they create?
2. Why might a person have a greater spiritual conflict after

becoming a Christian than before?

3. Are the legalist and the antinomian (see bottom of page 101 and top of page 102) still with us today? Are they found in the church? If so, what examples can you give of their teaching and influence?

4. Would we be better off if the law of God had never been given? Why or why not?

5. What counsel would you give if a new believer came and told you that since becoming a Christian he or she had been experiencing a terrible struggle with sin?

CHAPTER TWELVE

LIFE IN
THE SPIRIT

Romans 8:1-17

RAY STEDMAN tells of two magazine pictures he saw at the close of World War II that showed an infantryman in conflict with a tank. The first picture showed a gigantic tank bearing down on a tiny figure of a foot soldier. Obviously he had no defenses against the tank and would be crushed to death. When a soldier with nothing but a rifle faces a huge tank, the odds favor the tank. The second picture showed the same soldier, but now he was armed with a different weapon — a rocket launcher. In this picture the tank was smaller and the soldier had increased in size to be at least equal with, if not a little larger than, the tank. The different weapon radically increased his ability to counteract and defeat the opposing force of the tank.

At the close of Romans 7 it seems as though the "tank" of the "flesh" has the upper hand in its continuous battle with the mind and spirit of the Christian. But in Romans 8 Paul turns the spotlight on a new weapon available to the Christian — the Holy Spirit. Romans 8 brings the Holy Spirit to the rescue of the embattled Christian in his war against the flesh. What we cannot do in our own power, the Holy Spirit does for us. When the Holy Spirit enters the picture in Romans 8, exultations of victory fill the air, and there is no more talk of defeat.

The Holy Spirit has been mentioned only twice so far in this epistle (Rom. 5:5 and 7:6). But here in this eighth chapter He

is referred to a total of 18 times (in the *NASB*). Paul usually
refers to Him as simply "the Spirit" (vv. 4-6, 9, 13, 16, 23, 26,
27). But he also calls Him the Spirit of life (v. 2), the Spirit of
God (vv. 9, 14), the Spirit of Christ (v. 9), the Spirit of Him
who raised Jesus from the dead (v. 11), His Spirit (v. 11), and
a Spirit of adoption (v. 15). Therefore, Romans 8 has often
been labeled, and rightly so, the Holy Spirit chapter of the
Bible. The work of the Holy Spirit is explained theologically
in this chapter in terms of liberation, aspiration, resurrection,
mortification, and adoption.

Liberation

The "therefore" of Romans 8:1 harkens back not only to the
immediate context, Romans 7:25a, but also to the broader context of the epistle. In fact, Romans 8:1-4 brings together the
two magnificent themes of the two previous sections of Romans, the themes of justification and sanctification, both of
which are the result of the ministry of Christ. "There is therefore now no condemnation for those who are **in Christ Jesus**"
(v. 1) is the justification theme. And "the law of the Spirit of
life **in Christ Jesus**" (v. 2) is the sanctification theme. Christ
is both our Justifier and our Sanctifier, and the two are inex-
tricably bound together. In both there is *liberation* for those
who are in Christ Jesus.

First there is liberation from condemnation. Condemnation
refers to the punishment which follows a sentence — in other
words, penal servitude. "There is no reason why those who are
'in Christ Jesus' should go on doing penal servitude as though
they had never been pardoned and never been liberated from
the prison-house of sin."[1]

This liberation is not a future event; it is the "now" experience of the Christian. Believers are under no condemnation
because the condemnation now rests on "sin in the flesh"
(v. 3). Jesus Christ liberated the Christian and put the sentence on sin. Paul had previously referred to himself as "a
prisoner of the law of sin" (7:23). But now, because of Christ,
both he and we have been set "free from the law of sin and of
death" (v. 2). Again, this liberation is not a future event, for
there is *now* no condemnation. Freedom from condemnation is
an experience to be enjoyed in this life, not just in heaven in
the future. Jesus Christ did what the law could not do. The
law's weakness was its lack of inherent power to change our

sin nature (the flesh). But where the law failed, God succeeded. How? By "sending His own Son in the likeness of sinful flesh and *as an offering* for sin" (v. 3).

The preciseness of Paul's language here is significant. Jesus
did not come "in sinful flesh," because His flesh was sinless.
Neither did Jesus come in the "likeness of flesh," because His
flesh was real. Rather, Jesus came "in the likeness of sinful
flesh" because His flesh was both sinless and real.

And why did God thus send His Son? "As an offering for
sin" (v. 3) supplies the answer (cf. II. Cor. 5:21). The Greek
phrase used here often has sacrificial overtones, but here the
meaning may be more general, that is, that Christ came to
deal with the entire problem of sin. At any rate, God's mission
of condemning sin and releasing us from condemnation was
carried out through the person and work of Jesus Christ.

The liberation theme continues in verse 4. As a result of the
work of Christ and the ministry of the Holy Spirit, we are
changed so dramatically that the righteous requirements of
the law can now be fulfilled in us. We are set free, liberated to
do what we could never do before, namely, obey the law.

In our flesh we could not obey the law. But now we can!
How? By constantly living (walking) according to the Spirit.
The Holy Spirit empowers us so that our conduct begins to
fulfill the holy requirements of the law. We could never do
that on our own. But now, through the Holy Spirit, the
prophecy of Ezekiel is fulfilled: "Moreover, I will give you a
new heart and put a new spirit within you; . . . And I will put
My Spirit within you and cause you to walk in My statutes,
and you will be careful to observe My ordinances" (Ezek.
36:26, 27). The righteous requirements of the law can be fulfilled in us only because God has given divine aid, the Holy
Spirit, to meet the divine requirements. The law could
command, but could not enable us. But because of the Holy
Spirit, we now have an Enabler who produces His fruit in our
lives.

> To run and work the law commands,
> Yet gives me neither feet nor hands;
> But better news that the gospel brings:
> It bids me fly and gives me wings.

As Christians our responsibility is to walk (continuously)
"according to the Spirit" (v. 4). Only then will Christian holi-

ness be produced in us by Him. Thus by the Holy Spirit we are liberated in a positive sense to bear the fruit of holiness, which we could never do without the power of the Holy Spirit.

Aspiration

The second ministry of the Holy Spirit deals with Christian aspiration, that is, where our minds are focused. This paragraph (vv. 5-9) develops in the form of antithetical parallelism, a form found frequently in the wisdom literature of the Old Testament. The contrast — which is between the "flesh" (the sin nature) and "the Spirit" — actually begins in the last part of verse 4, which speaks of walking (living) according to the flesh or according to the Spirit. In verses 5-9 Paul develops this contrast in terms of human aspirations, the results of those aspirations, the futility of the flesh, and the way out of the flesh.

From the way Paul excludes the Romans from being "in the flesh" (v. 9), we can infer that he is using the term "flesh" to refer to the unregenerate nature and that he is using the term Spirit to refer to the Holy Spirit who has regenerated them through the life-giving event of the new birth. In verse 5 Paul makes a statement about those who have the flesh as their essential nature and those who have the Spirit. He continues to show that there is a definite connection between a person's being and the things that interest that person. The fleshly nature sets its mind on fleshly things. The Spirit-inspired nature sets its mind on the things of the Spirit.

Conversely, the things we aspire to reveal our essential nature. The point of Romans 7:14-25 was that the person who lives according to the flesh cannot live according to the Spirit. Romans 8 expresses the other side, that the person who lives according to the Spirit cannot live according to the flesh. The verb translated "set their minds on" (v. 5) has both the flesh and the Spirit as its subject and predicate. The Greek word is expansive in that it expresses not only *thinking* but *willing*. It describes not only mental activity but also the deliberate directing of the mind to something. John R.W. Stott says, "It is a question of our preoccupations, the ambitions which compel us and the interests which engross us; how we spend our time, money and energy; what we give ourselves up to."[2]

So the expression "set their minds on" includes not only concentration of thought, but also our desires and our aspira-

tions. These two "mind-sets" have radically different consequences. Death is the result for the fleshly minded ("carnally
minded," *KJV*), while life and peace are the results for the
person who directs his aspirations on the things of the Spirit.
While sin produces death (6:23), the Spirit brings forth life
and peace.

The Greek language has two words for life. One refers to
biological life, which ends with physical death. The other refers to the principle of life. The second is the word used here
(v. 6). For the Christian, the principle of life is none other
than the Holy Spirit Himself. He is the life of God in the soul
of man. This life is the very life of God communicated to believers by the Holy Spirit. He is the life-giving Spirit.

The mind set on the Spirit has peace, but the mind set on
the flesh is hostile toward God (v. 7). The flesh is in rebellion
against God's law, which it finds impossible to obey. Therefore, those who are in the flesh cannot please God, because
they are always disobeying His law. Obviously God is not
pleased by disobedience. Notice the sharp contrast between
the flesh and the Spirit regarding the law of God (vv. 4, 7). In
summary, our essential nature (flesh or Spirit) determines
our aspirations. And our aspirations determine our relationship to God — either death or life.

After stating these general principles, Paul applies them to
his readers (v. 9). He knows that they are not in the flesh
because they are in the Spirit. As Christian believers they
have the Spirit, who alone is the antidote for the flesh. They
are in the Spirit because the Spirit of God now indwells them.
A new resident now motivates and empowers them. Indwelling sin (7:17, 20) has been displaced by the indwelling Spirit
of God. This is the only way that a person can move from
"flesh" to "Spirit": "you are . . . in the Spirit, if indeed the
Spirit of God dwells in you" (v. 9). The "if indeed" could also
be translated "provided that," and indicates that the Holy
Spirit, here called the Spirit of God, is the only agent of spiritual regeneration. That which is born of the Spirit is spirit
(Jn. 3:6).

The "Spirit of God" and "the Spirit of Christ" in this verse
are synonymous with the Holy Spirit. Since the Holy Spirit
baptizes each believer into the body of Christ (I Cor. 12:13),
Paul declares that one cannot be a member of Christ's body
unless he has the Spirit of Christ. According to Galatians

2:20, Christ in a sense becomes the new "I" of the redeemed person. Belonging to Him is an established fact. Therefore the Christian's aspirations are Christ-directed and will naturally be set on the things of the Spirit.

Resurrection

The third ramification of life in the Spirit is resurrection. Earlier Paul wrote of being united with Christ in His resurrection (6:3-11), but at that point he made no mention of the Holy Spirit. Now he presents the Holy Spirit as the one who raised Jesus from the dead and points to what it means for the Christian to have the Spirit of the resurrection dwelling in him (v. 11). The ramifications are both spiritual and physical.

Experientially, the Holy Spirit's work of regeneration in our *spirits* precedes His resurrection work in our mortal *bodies*. But since the Spirit who now dwells in the Christian is the same Spirit who raised Jesus from the dead, the resurrection of our physical bodies is guaranteed. The same spiritual power that raised Jesus from the dead is given to all those who believe (Eph. 1:19-20).

Paul has already called the Holy Spirit the "Spirit of Life." As such He was the Life-Giver in creation (Gen. 1:2). He is the Life-Giver in the new birth (Jn. 3:5). He is the Life-Giver in sanctification, as He brings an end to the tyranny of the sin nature and its consequence — death. And here He is presented as the Life-Giver not only in Christ's resurrection, but also in ours. He will also give life to our mortal bodies. Our bodies became mortal, i.e., subject to death (v. 10), because of sin. As a result the process of physical decay works daily in our bodies. But this should not cause us to become discouraged, for "though our outer man is decaying, yet our inner man is being renewed day by day" (II Cor. 4:16). The Holy Spirit is the agent of this present spiritual renewal of the Christian, and He will also be the agent of the future physical renewal when we receive our new glorified bodies in the resurrection. "The presence of the Spirit in the redeemed life is at once the evidence of salvation bestowed and the earnest of that final phase of salvation that belongs to the future (v. 11)."[3]

Notice the close connection between Christ and the Holy Spirit. In verse 10, Christ in us makes our spirits alive because of righteousness — His righteousness imputed to us. In verse 11 it is "His Spirit who indwells you." The same Spirit who lived in Christ also lives in the Christian, and, as a result, our spirits come alive. The Holy Spirit gives you the very life of God, blessedly spiritual and indestructibly eternal, and you have this life *now*, "if Christ is in you" (v. 10). This immediately brings us to the fourth aspect of the Spirit's victorious work in the Christian.

Mortification

That the mortification theme is a logical corollary to the resurrection theme is indicated by the transition words, "So then, brethren, we are under obligation . . ." (v. 12). Paul states our obligation in negative terms. Because the Holy Spirit now indwells us, we have no obligation to the sin nature. We owe it no allegiance whatsoever. Instead of following the dictates of the sin nature, which result in death, Christians are empowered **by the Spirit** to "mortify the deeds of the body" (v. 13, *KJV*).

The sinful nature in the Christian has not been eradicated, but we are under no obligation to it. Quite the contrary, we attack it through the new power of the Spirit. In Romans 7:23 Paul complained about the activity of the law of sin, which was at work in the members of his body. At that point the law of sin had the upper hand because Paul, as is often the case with many Christians, tried to fight the battle himself. But now, through the Spirit, he will mortify the deeds of the body.

The meaning of the word mortify has changed. For us it communicates excessive embarrassment. We say, "I was mortified," as we tell our friend about an extremely embarrassing thing that happened to us. But in this verse (v. 13) the word means "to put to death, destroy, render extinct." "*Mortification* (putting to death by the power of the Spirit the deeds of the body) means a ruthless rejection of all practices we know to be wrong: a daily repentance, turning from all known sins of habit, practice, association or thought. . . . The only attitude to adopt towards the flesh is to kill it."[4]

Ralph Earle offers this clarification: "Paul is not here pleading for a rigorous asceticism. He is not advocating the suppression of all physical desires and the denial of any enjoyment of physical pleasure. What he is saying is that all the bodily activities carried on independently of the Spirit and in defiance of His dominion should be put to death"[5] This putting to death of the deeds of the body (mortification) must be the constant, unremittingly maintained approach of the Christian toward the sin nature, and we do this *by the Spirit* who indwells us. That's the only way we can constantly mortify the deeds of the body.

Adoption

This magnificent passage reaches a victorious climax as we learn that the Spirit who indwells us is a spirit of adoption, who makes us nothing less than the sons and daughters of God. Under the law, the highest relationship with God a person may attain is servitude, which is inevitably accompanied by "a spirit of slavery leading to fear" (v. 15). But under grace, Christians are accepted into a filial relationship of love characterized by the joyous and grateful obedience of those who have become members of the family. Paul develops this same theme in Galatians 4:1-7.

There are several advantages which come to Christians as a result of adoption. The first is suggested by the word adoption itself. "The term 'adoption' may smack somewhat of artificiality in our ears; but in the first century AD an adopted son was a son deliberately chosen by his adoptive father to perpetuate his name and inherit his estate; he was no whit inferior in status to a son born in the ordinary course of nature, and might well enjoy the father's affection more fully and reproduce the father's character more worthily"[6]

What marvelous grace! God has deliberately chosen us, sinners though we be, and elevated us to the status of sons (Eph. 1:3-6).

Second, we have a constant guide, the Spirit of God, who will lead us through this life. The story is told of a certain guide who lived in the deserts of Arabia who never got lost. What was his secret? He always carried a homing pigeon with a very fine cord attached to its legs. When he was in doubt about which path to take, the guide would throw the pigeon into flight, keeping hold on the line. The pigeon would always fly in the direction of home and in this way lead the guide to his destination. Because of his unique method, this guide became known as "the dove man." As children of God, we have the Heavenly Dove to guide us through the pilgrimage of this life to our heavenly home. This truth is captured in the following words from a Christian hymn:

Holy Spirit, faithful Guide,
Ever near the Christian's side;
Gently lead us by the hand,
Pilgrims in a desert land; . . .
                                                    Wells

Third, as adopted children we come into a new relationship with God. We now know Him as Father. He is the kind of Father who loves his children perfectly. As a result, all fear is removed from our lives (v. 15; cf. I Jn. 4:18). God, as Father, opens Himself to such an intimate relationship with us that we can call him by the same name Jesus used, "Abba" (cf. Mk. 14:36). "Abba" (cf. Gal. 4:6) was the Aramaic term for father. It indicated the kind of intimate relationship between a father and his children that our word "Daddy" represents. Because of the indwelling Spirit, we can know God so well that we can call Him "Daddy." This kind of intimacy has such a dynamic quality of respect, however, that we must never allow it to degenerate into flippancy on our part.

Attestation is the fourth advantage of this new relationship which we have as members of God's family. "The Spirit himself testifies with our spirit that we are God's children" (v. 16, *NIV*). John Wesley wrote that the witness of God's Spirit "is an inward impression on the soul, whereby the Spirit of God directly witnesses to my spirit, that I am a child of God; that Jesus Christ hath loved me, and given himself for me; and that all my sins are blotted out, and I, even I, am reconciled to God." The human spirit receives this attestation from the Holy Spirit and corroborates it. Wesley continues, "Strictly speaking, it is a conclusion drawn partly from the word of God, and partly from our own experience. The word of God says, every one who has the fruit of the Spirit is a child of God; experience, or inward consciousness, tells me, that I have the fruit of the Spirit; and hence I rationally conclude, 'Therefore I am a child of God' "[7]

The fifth blessed advantage of adoption is that we become "heirs of God and fellow-heirs with Christ" (v. 17; cf. Gal. 4:7). Since we are now adopted into the family of God, we become heirs to everything God is, and our inheritance is the same as that of *the* Son of God, Jesus Christ. The glory which we Christians will inherit by grace is the same glory which is His by right (see Jn. 17:22-24).

Since we are coheirs with Jesus, the pathway to our inheri-

tance will be the same as His. Before we will share in the fullness of His glory, we must first share in His sufferings. Everything about the Christian life is identification with Christ.
Since we now, through adoption, share His sonship, we shall
also share His inheritance in glory. But first we must share
His sufferings. If we don't bear the cross, then we can't wear
the crown. In this same vein Paul elsewhere spoke of knowing
Christ, not only in the power of His resurrection, but also in
the "fellowship of His sufferings" (Phil. 3:10).

But suffering is not the final word. God's grace through
Jesus Christ transforms suffering so that it is not a dead end.
Now, through Christ, it becomes a means to God's redemptive
goal — the restoration of His glory in His highest creation,
human beings. If we share His sufferings, we will also share
His glory (cf. II. Cor. 4:10, 11).

Life in the Spirit is a life of victory made personal in the
experience of every Christian who will live by the power of
the Holy Spirit. In such Christians the Holy Spirit is at work
providing liberation, a new aspiration, resurrection, mortification, adoption (and in the next paragraph of Romans 8,
glorification). Surely, no Christian would want to shun these
"_____ tions" of the Spirit! Through them God's work of
justification and sanctification reaches its pinnacle. "Thanks
be to God through Jesus Christ our Lord!" (Rom. 7:25).

QUESTIONS FOR DISCUSSION

1. Do you think the church today puts enough emphasis on
   sanctification? Give reasons for your answer.
2. How are both Christ and the Holy Spirit involved in the
   Christian's liberation?
3. How does a Christian walk "according to the Spirit"? Is it
   an automatic process, or does it require effort? Explain
   your answer.
4. What are the blessings of being adopted into God's family?
   What are the responsibilities?
5. In the light of this chapter, why do so many Christians
   still fail to live victorious Christian lives?

CHAPTER THIRTEEN

MORE THAN CONQUERORS

Romans 8:18-39

IN the last part of chapter 8, Paul concludes the first half of his letter to the Romans with a lofty and exuberant melody, as he combines the inspiring notes of the future glory and the present experience of Christians, both of which are the results of God's saving work. Paul's statement in verse 37, "But in all these things we overwhelmingly conquer through Him who loved us," expresses both the pinnacle of Christian victory and the means by which that victory is achieved.

In this verse the Greek word for conquer has the prefix from which our word "hyper" is derived. Hyper refers to that which is beyond the ordinary, as in hyperactive, hypersensitive, hyperbole, etc. Thus Paul declares that we are hyperconquerors. Our victory in Christ is more than an ordinary victory. It is extraordinary!

Over the past several years a game has been played in the National Football League every January. Known as the Super Bowl, it pits the two best football teams in a showdown game. At the end of that game, one team is called the loser. But how can that team, the second best team in all of football, be considered a loser? Really, they are not so much losers as the winners are super winners. The winners are more than conquerors. They are hyperconquerors.

The victory which Christ has earned and which He shares with those who believe in Him is the ultimate victory, a victory which need never be topped. His victory far surpasses even our most aspiring and inspiring hopes and our loftiest imaginings (Eph. 3:20). Thus in Christ we are hyperconquerors, both in the present and in the eternal future. In this section Paul describes how being a hyperconqueror changes our perspective on suffering (vv. 18-27), and he elucidates three of the underlying reasons why we are hyperconquerors (vv. 28-39).

A Different Perspective on Suffering

If you have ever had your eyes examined by an optometrist, you are familiar with the instrument he places in front of your eyes, an instrument with many different lenses which he uses to test your vision. In this chapter Paul uses several different lenses to explain one of the most baffling experiences in human existence, the experience of suffering. He expands our understanding of suffering by helping us view it through three different lenses.

The first is the lens of glory (v. 18). All present suffering must be viewed from the perspective of the Christian's future glory. Paul did not write from an ivory tower. He had suffered many times in many different ways (read II Cor. 11:23-33). Many Christians, if they endured such things, would begin to question God and would become discouraged and bitter, wondering why a dedicated servant of Christ should experience so much suffering.

But there was neither self-pity nor doubt with Paul, because he saw beyond all these things to the glory that is to be revealed to us. When he compared the promised glory with his present sufferings, the sufferings became insignificant.

To understand Paul's comparison, picture a balance scale similar to one used at a candy counter. If you ask for a pound of candy, the clerk puts a pound weight on one side. Then she fills the container on the other side with candy until its weight balances with the pound weight.

Paul says, "Put all your present sufferings on one side of the scale and watch it drop from all that weight. But that is not the complete picture. To get a proper perspective on suffering, place the glory yet to be revealed to us on the other side of the scale. When you do that, it will far surpass even the most intense suffering you will endure in this present age."

Read II Corinthians 4:16-18, where Paul presents a similar

contrast between affliction and glory. The affliction is *light* when compared with the *weight* of glory. The present affliction is *momentary*, even if it lasts a whole lifetime, but the glory is *eternal*. The affliction will end, but the glory will last forever. To have a proper view of suffering, we must see it through the lens of glory.

The Lens of Creation

Second, we also need to look at suffering through the lens of creation (vv. 19-22). Here Paul personifies creation in order to vividly describe the bondage which it has experienced since the fall of man and woman in the Garden of Eden. At that time the ground was cursed (Gen. 3:17), and the beautiful harmony of creation became discord. Since then creation has experienced what scientists call the second law of thermodynamics. Because of an infinite increase in entropy, there is an irreversible tendency of a system, including the universe, toward disorder. Paul describes creation as having been "subjected to futility" (v. 20) and in "slavery to corruption" (v. 21).

The natural creation is frustrated. It was designed to produce beautiful flowers and luscious food naturally. But now, because of the curse, thorns and weeds are its products. Hurricanes, tornadoes, and earthquakes are results of a frustrated natural order. Because of all this "the whole creation groans" (v. 22). The German poet Goethe said that nature seemed to him to be like a captive maiden crying aloud for release. Someone else observed that many of the sounds of nature (e.g., the sighing of the wind) are in a minor key. Human beings also experience the futility, the emptiness, the winding down, the decay, and the groaning.

Seeing all of this, are we to agree with the preacher in Ecclesiastes, who cried out, "Vanity of vanities! All is vanity!"? Although so much of the pain seems meaningless, it is not. It is as purposeful as the pain of childbirth (v. 22). Because of God's redemptive work, "these groans portend life, not death. They are full of hope, not despair. They are the pangs of birth, not the throes of death. Out of the agony of the present the new heavens and earth are being born."[1]

The pains of childbirth are severe, but they produce life. The curse upon creation will be removed when the process of redemption is completed at the revealing of the sons of God.

Therefore creation joins with us in eagerly awaiting the time when our salvation will be completed with the redemption of our bodies (v. 23). Though creation continues to suffer, God's redemptive work is so complete that its suffering will one day cease. On that day there will be streams in the desert and it will blossom profusely. On that day the hostility now in the natural creation will be removed, so that the lion — no longer ferocious — will lie down with the lamb.

The Lens of the Spirit

Third, Paul looks at suffering through the lens of the Spirit (vv. 23-27). Though we suffer, we do not despair. We are sustained by hope. We eagerly look forward to experiencing our completed inheritance. We know this hope for the future is certain because of the Spirit's presence in our lives now, as a "first fruit" (v. 23).

In the Old Testament, Israel was commanded to give the first of every harvest to God. They could joyfully and thankfully give Him the first fruits because they believed that the rest of the harvest would be bountiful, as He had promised. God has promised to complete our redemption by removing the curse of sin not only from our spirits and minds, but also from our physical bodies. Though we are now the children of God by adoption, one day our adoption will be complete, when our bodies are transformed into ones like that of our glorified Lord (Phil. 3:20, 21).

The Holy Spirit's presence in our lives now is God's guarantee that this hope is not a pipe dream. We eagerly await (standing on tiptoe, stretching our necks, as at an airport trying to catch the first glimpse of an arriving passenger we are eager to see after many years' absence) the day when hope will be replaced by fulfillment. In the meantime the Holy Spirit helps us in our weakness, as we groan through this time of suffering, so that we persevere until the time of fulfillment.

The Spirit does this by being our divine prayer partner (vv. 26-27). C.H. Dodd defined prayer as "the Divine in us appealing to the Divine above us." This is possible only because of the ministry of the indwelling Spirit. We need help because we are weak. He is the strength that we need. Specifically, He intercedes for us at times when we are not sure what to pray. At times like that, if we had no help, our prayer life would cease. Sometimes life can be so confusing and our understand-

ing of God's will so limited that we do not know what to pray.
Sometimes we want to pray but are so burdened that verbal
expression is impossible. Yet at these times we need prayer
the most. Praise God, because of the Spirit our prayer contact
remains active in spite of our weakness. Prayer includes lis-
tening to the Spirit as He prays for us. He is infinite and
knows clearly the will of God for every circumstance. By following His lead, we can pray according to the will of God.
(First John 5:14, 15 tells why this is important.)

Several years ago I visited a devout Christian lady. As we
talked about prayer, she told me of one of her experiences.
Her husband worked from 11:00 p.m. to 7:00 a.m. in a railroad switching yard. One morning she woke at three o'clock
with the distinct impression that she should pray. Since she
had no idea of the specific need, she did not know what to
pray. But in obedience to the Spirit, she arose and knelt by
her bed. No words came, but she groaned and sobbed in a
spirit of prayer, allowing the Spirit to pray "with groanings
too deep for words" (v. 26). In time the groanings ceased, and
she went back to bed.

When the woman's husband arrived home later that day, he
told her that he had nearly been crushed when he fell between two railroad cars as they were being switched. She
asked what time it happened. "At three a.m.," he replied. In
her human finiteness, this woman had not known what to
pray; but the Spirit interceded.

Through the Holy Spirit we can communicate with God
even during this present age, which is characterized by suffering and weakness. Because of the indwelling Spirit, when we
are weak we are strong, because His strength takes the place
of our weakness. Therefore, we are hyperconquerors.

Hyperconquerors Because of God's Eternal Purpose

Having considered how being a hyperconqueror changes our
perspective on suffering, Paul proceeds in verses 28-30 to give
the first of three reasons why we are hyperconquerors. It is
because God's eternal purpose has been that we be more than
conquerors. God fulfills this purpose in spite of problems and
difficulties. God is at work transforming even the horrendous
things in our lives into good. Man's evil placed Jesus Christ
on the cross, but God transformed His crucifixion into good —
our salvation. "Everything that happens to you, ever will hap-

pen, that is happening now, however tragic, however difficult, however impossible, however hopeless, however inexplicable, in everything that has happened God leads in victory to his own glory and to your eternal benefit"[2]

Verse 28 nullifies coincidence, for God is the One who works for the good of those who love Him. He uses not just the good things, but all things.

Recently in New York City a magnificent carpet sold for 25 thousand dollars. Imported from Turkey, it contained over 100 delicate shades and hues. Amazingly, this beautiful masterpiece was actually made up of 11,877,000 knots! This is a picture of God's work in a Christian's life. By His wise providence God takes what we may perceive to be only a series of interminable tangles, snarls, and knots, places them in His divine shuttle, and produces a pattern of beauty that will last for eternity. We will become disappointed and discouraged with the process of life if we lose sight of the final product, which God in his eternal purpose is creating.

Verses 29-30 give the specifics of God's purpose and how He accomplishes it. The word translated "foreknew" is the root for our word prognosis. Even before God created the world, He knew what was going to happen. He knew that man would rebel against Him, so He also formulated a plan of salvation before He created anything else. From all eternity God's purpose and grace designed our salvation in Jesus Christ (II Tim. 1:9). "Predestined" focuses on God's initiative and is His gracious act without which salvation would be impossible. The word is used four other times in the New Testament (Acts 4:28; I Cor. 2:7; Eph. 1:5 and 11), and it never speaks of someone being predestined to hell. Man chooses that himself. Instead, notice that we are specifically predestined to Christlikeness.

Visitors today at the Cathedral at Cologne see two seemingly identical pictures of the crucifixion of Peter hanging side by side. In the early 19th century Napoleon ransacked the city and took the original painting from the cathedral. After his masterpiece was stolen, the artist created another from memory. Later the original was recovered, restored, and displayed beside the second painting. There is so little difference between the two that one can hardly tell which was painted first.

Spiritually speaking, the Original, Jesus Christ, is absent, for He is now in heaven. But God's plan is to create the likeness of Jesus Christ in the life of every Christian. That's the purpose of predestination.

God's activity continued through "calling" and "justification" and culminates in future "glorification." All of the main verbs in verses 29-30, including "glorified," are in the tense that indicates completed action. The Christian's glorification — the completion of our salvation — though still future for us is a completed event in the purpose of God. Therefore its happening is certain.

The five affirmations of these verses are like a chain with five unbreakable links that stretch from eternity past to eternity future. "God is pictured as moving steadily on from stage to stage — from an eternal foreknowledge and predestination, through an historical call and justification, to a final glorification of His people in heaven."[3] In the light of all this divine activity on our behalf, no wonder Paul declares that we are hyperconquerors. Such is God's purpose.

Hyperconquerors Because God Is For Us

Verses 31-34 give the second reason Christians are hyperconquerors — God is for us — with its accompanying conclusion that, therefore, no one can be against us. Paul asks us to begin to draw some practical conclusions from what he has already written by asking, "What then shall we say to these things?" What "things" is he talking about? Think back over the preceding verses of Romans 8: There is no condemnation for those who are in Christ. We are set free from the law of sin and death. What the law couldn't do, God did in sending His Son, Jesus Christ into our lives. He has given us the mind of the Spirit, which results in life and peace for us. He has given us the Spirit, who indwells us as Christians. He has given us the Spirit in whom there is life. He has given us the same Spirit who raised Jesus Christ from the dead. As a result we are the sons of God. We are led by the Spirit. We have the spirit of adoption making us a part of God's family. The Spirit bears witness to our spirit that we are the children of God. The Spirit has been given to us as the pledge of the future glory that is to come. God has guaranteed through the Spirit the redemption of our physical bodies. The Holy Spirit ministers to us when we in our weakness don't know how to pray as we should, so that we can still pray through our divine Prayer

Partner. He causes all things to work together to good for those who love Him. All of this, and more.

What shall we say to *these* things? There's only one conclusion we can reach. Beyond any shadow of a doubt, God has demonstrated that He is for us. God is on our side. The question is not simply, "Who is against us?" Certainly many people and things are against us: sin, death, Satan, unbelievers, etc. But the question is prefaced by the statement, "If [Since] God is for us. . . ." That certainly handles any and all obstacles. God Himself is our champion and defender. Therefore, and only on this basis, are we hyperconquerors.

Paul continues by asking a series of questions (vv. 32-35) designed to reinforce the truth that God is on our side. God has already given the ultimate gift. At great cost to Himself, He gave His only Son (Jn. 3:16; Rom. 5:8). Having given us the very best, He will not be stingy with other, less significant gifts. The cross of Jesus Christ vividly demonstrates God's generosity toward us and powerfully declares that God is on our side. If we have the Christ of the cross and the gift of eternal life He there provided, what more do we need?

Verses 33 and 34 take us into a courtroom. Who can bring a charge against us? Even the accusations of Satan fall on deaf ears, for the guilty have already been sentenced and pardoned. Jesus bore the penalty and, as a result, we are pardoned. Because we are pardoned, who can condemn us? Do you remember Romans 8:1? On the basis of His all-sufficient sacrificial death and victorious resurrection, Jesus continues to serve as our Great High Priest by interceding for us and serving as our defense attorney in the courts of heaven. Christ won for us the victory over the penalty and the power of sin and protects that victory in our lives daily. All this proves that God is not our adversary. Rather, He is our redeemer and defender. Therefore, we are hyperconquerors.

Hyperconquerors Because of God's Tenacious Love

In verse 35 Paul asks the last in a series of questions that began in verse 31. With this question he gives the third reason that Christians are hyperconquerors: "Who shall separate us from the love of Christ?" Paul suggests several possible answers to this question in verses 35, 38, and 39. His list includes the toughest things that people can face in their lives. Paul himself had experienced everything mentioned in verse 35, and many of the Roman Christians to whom he was writing would soon endure tribulation and persecution as well.

When Christians experience suffering, difficulties, adversities, and setbacks, we must not conclude that these things have any power to separate us from God's love. His love is tenacious. His lovingkindness is eternal, for it is one of the attributes of the eternal God. Even when we seem to be as helpless as sheep about to be slaughtered, God's love is drawing us to Himself for eternity. Though we may be hard pressed by hostile forces, God's love preserves our eternal spirits. We should not fear those things that harm the body, for our bodies are only temporal. Instead, we should be concerned about those things that harm our eternal spirits.

The things listed in verses 38-39 are even more awesome than those listed in verse 35. Death, of course, is a dreaded menace, but even here God has given us victory. "Life" itself can be so tough that some prefer death to life. But God provides assurance and hope, so that life need not conquer us. "Principalities" probably include both Satanic powers and earthly governmental authorities. "Things present," no matter how severe — loss of health, home, employment, etc. — need not destroy us. God's love gives a foundation from which we can begin to cope. "Things to come" — some fear the future and all its potential for accelerated adversity, but the eternal God will be there too. "Height" and "depth" may refer to the astrological beliefs of some that their lives were controlled by the configuration of the stars. But God's love also goes with us through all the ups and downs of life. None of these things, no matter how powerful they are, have any ability to separate a Christian from God's love, which is in Jesus Christ our Lord.

Romans 8 ends as it began — "in Jesus Christ" (cf. v. 1). He is victor. Only in Him are we hyperconquerors. Without Him we are totally defeated. He is **Lord** over life and death, for He was crucified and raised from the dead. He is Lord over all principalities and powers, for He triumphed over them in His cross (Col. 2:15). He is Lord of things present and things to come, for it is in Him that God chose us in love and it is in Him that we shall enter into God's final glory. Having listed the most powerful enemies that attack the Christian, Paul sees that all of them are ultimately powerless (as long as we stay in Christ Jesus and honor Him as Lord) to destroy our relationship with God based on his tenacious love.

We Christians are not defeated. Not even the gates of hell can prevail against us. The gospel according to Paul is a message of triumph that gives birth to a victorious Christian life that has its source in the Victor. All foes are impotent. We are members of the church triumphant. Nothing can drive a wedge between the Savior and His love for His redeemed people. Paul exudes confidence. It's not a superficial self-confidence, but a genuine God-confidence. Christians are excessively victorious through Jesus Christ. "Thanks be to God, who gives us the victory through our Lord Jesus Christ" (I Cor. 15:57). Because of Him and only because of Him, we are hyperconquerors.

QUESTIONS FOR DISCUSSION

1. Why do we have trouble seeing beyond the present suffering to the future glory?
2. How does the Holy Spirit help us in our prayer life? Have you ever had an experience of groaning in the Spirit?
3. What perspective have you gained from this chapter on some of the problems and difficulties you have experienced in your life? Can you see God's hand at work in these experiences?
4. Do you think that some Christians have trouble believing that "God is for us"? If so, why? How has God shown that He is "on our side"?
5. What changes do you think might take place in our churches if most Christians became convinced that we are indeed superconquerors and then acted on that belief?

NOTES

Introduction
1. Everett F. Harrison, "Romans," *The Expositor's Bible Commentary* (Grand Rapids: Zondervan, 1976), Vol. 10, p. 5.

Chapter 2
1. Tim LaHaye, *The Battle for the Mind* (Old Tappan, N.J.: Fleming H. Revell, 1980), p. 96.
2. Quoted by Ray Stedman in a sermon originally preached on December 14, 1975, in Palo Alto, Calif., and later printed.
3. Steve Turner, *Nice and Nasty* (Manchester, England: Marshall, Morgan, and Scott).

Chapter 5
1. Harrison, *op. cit.*, p. 39.
2. F.F. Bruce, *The Epistle of Paul to the Romans (The Tyndale New Testament Commentaries)* (Grand Rapids: Eerdmans, 1963), pp. 102-3.
3. Harrison, *op. cit.*, p. 43.
4. Bruce, *op. cit.*, p. 108.

Chapter 8
1. H.W. Byrne, *A Christian Approach to Education* (Grand Rapids: Zondervan, 1961), p. 51. Used by permission.
2. Richard C. Halverson, *Prologue to Prison* (Los Angeles: Cowman Publishing Co., 1964), pp. 123-4.
3. Robert Haldane, *An Exposition of the Epistle to the Romans* (Mac Dill AFB, Fla.: Mac Donald Publishing Co., n.d.), p. 212.
4. Harrison, *op. cit.*, p. 65.

Chapter 9
1. Harrison, *op. cit.*, p. 70.
2. John R.W. Stott, *Men Made New* (Downers Grove, Ill.: Inter-Varsity Press, 1966), pp. 49-50. (The passage is not a quotation, but a summation of Stott's ideas.)

Chapter 10
1. F.F. Bruce, *op. cit.*, pp. 142-3.
2. Harrison, *op. cit.*, p. 66.

Chapter 11
1. Stott, *op. cit.*, pp. 59-60.

2. Watchman Nee, *The Normal Christian Life* (London: Witness and Testimony, 1959), pp. 109-10.

3. Stott, *op. cit.*, p. 76.

Chapter 12

1. Bruce, *op. cit.*, p. 159.

2. Stott, *op. cit.*, p. 87.

3. Harrison, *op. cit.*, p. 90.

4. Stott, *op. cit.*, p. 91

5. Ralph Earle, *Word Meanings in the New Testament* (Grand Rapids: Baker, 1974), Vol. III, pp. 152-3.

6. Bruce, *op. cit.*, p. 166.

7. Quoted by William M. Greathouse in "Romans," *Beacon Bible Commentary* (Kansas City: Beacon Hill Press, 1970), Vol. VIII, p. 176.

Chapter 13

1. F.B. Meyer, *Our Daily Homily* (Westwood, N.J.: Fleming H. Revell, 1966), p. 416.

2. Halverson, *op. cit.*, p. 182.

3. Stott, *op. cit.*, p. 102.

PERSONAL NOTES

Date Due

AUG 9 1987			